# Spinners

**Sylvester Nemes**

With entomological assistance by
Dr. Daniel Gustafson, Research Scientist,
Biology Department, Montana State University

STACKPOLE
BOOKS

Published by
STACKPOLE BOOKS
5067 Ritter Road
Mechanicsburg, PA 17055
www.stackpolebooks.com



Printed in the United States

10 9 8 7 6 5 4 3 2 1

# Contents

# Introduction and acknowledgements

This is the first book on fly fishing which deals solely with mayfly spinners. The book was meant to be thicker, but after three years, I began to see that there was a redundancy in the specimens I was gathering and in the artificial patterns I was trying to design. The spinners, I began to notice, were basically the same no matter how big or small; and no matter where they came from. (What did I expect when I started the work? Spinners with horns? Spinners with teeth? Spinners with no tails?)

Spinners from a public bath in an outdoor Roman ruin in France, and from an angling spring creek in the same country were no different, except for size and color from those taken in the East Gallatin River, four miles from my home in Bozeman, Montana. I also collected spinners in Michigan and Pennsylvania and they were no different from those in Montana, Idaho, and Yellowstone Park, the principal areas covered in this book. Some genera, Baetis among them, are world wide, so one could find the same spinner (and the artificial fly fishing pattern to imitate it, if there were fly fishing to be had) in the Rocky mountains as well as the Carpathian mountains in eastern Europe.

Spending another year or two collecting the insects, I felt, would be spinning my wheels. Most of the well-known mayfly spinners are covered in the book. And if the reader fishes his favorite cluster of streams in a certain area, he will know what mayflies will be up at certain times of the fishing season and should be able to tie the correct spinner imitations from the information in the book.

Publishers, I feel, should give more brains to their readers. They don't need profuse tables and charts which in the highly unpredictable world of insect life, do not mean much anyway. So, this book is without 'handy,' 'convenient,' 'complete', 'timesaving,' charts or tables showing mating dates, or 'spinner fall' dates and times. As I tried to point out in one of the chapters, dun emergence dates and times can be predicted more accurately than corresponding spinner activities because of the relative constancy of the water world in which the nymph lives and from which the dun hatches. Once in the air or 'outside' the relative safety of his water world, the mayfly, as a dun or as a spinner, is subjected to vagaries of the weather which can prevent the dun from ever becoming a spinner, or prevent the spinner from ever becoming a progenitor. Recorded in the book, for example, is an instance when Baetis duns never molted into spinners in 5 days because of bad weather, but would have normally molted into spinners in a day or less; and the appearance of one kind of spinner on a certain river suffering from severe drought, where it, the spinner, had never been seen before.

Spinners are also far more elusive than duns. Many anglers are aware of this and in March, 1993, I told George Lenzi, a French fly fisherman, I was working on this book and he asked me with a polite smile how long I thought I was going to live.

There can never be as many spinners as there are duns and it may be because of this that spinner fishing is not important to American anglers. Another obvious reason is that spinner fly imitations are difficult to see and many fly fishers will not fish a dry fly if they can't see it. Duns suffer tremendous tolls from fish and birds and other insects. If the weather turns bad after their emergence, duns can freeze to death or drown in a rain storm while waiting their designated time to turn into spinners.

The act of molting, itself, is fraught with peril and risk, and many duns perish at the last moment because their new spinner wings or much longer tails are not entirely clear of the dun exuviae which covered them. Spinners must fly and fly long and keenly in the act of copulation and freed, perfect wings and tails are primary to the task.

Just because this is the first book solely dedicated to spinners doesn't mean the subject of spinners is not covered in American fly fishing literature. Nearly every magazine has at least one article a year devoted to them. The 'hatch' books, SELECTIVE TROUT, 1971; HATCHES, 1975; MEETING AND FISHING THE HATCHES, 1977; MAYFLIES, THE ANGLER, AND THE TROUT, 1980; and THE COMPLETE BOOK OF WESTERN HATCHES, 1981; have all included spinner species, identifications and spinner imitations. Yet, and I think most readers would agree, that the emphasis in the 'hatch' books has been on the duns. As a result, many fly fishers today, believe the life cycle of the mayfly might begin with the nymph and end with the dun.

There is also a relative similarity in the spinner patterns from one book to the next, including a preponderance of dubbed bodies and poly wings. The method of tying spinner wings in this book is new and different, yet relatively easy. It is based on the writing and spinner designs of two earlier writers, Vincent Marinaro and Roger Woolley, both of whom used hackle fibers for the wings. Essentially, the hackles were wound around the head of the hook, then figure-eighted into the two sides. This is a tricky, and difficult manuever and I could not master it sufficiently, myself. In my method, the hackle is wound around the head of the hook, divided fifty-fifty and physically bent, pulled and flattened with thumbs and forefingers into the left and right hand sides. That's all. I was never able to find that method described anywhere, so I have legally trade-marked it and the flies.

Bodies of real spinners are thin and smooth with a see-through quality which I believe cannot be imitated with thickish dubbing, and not much better, really, with any other material. In smaller sized spinner patterns, it is virtually impossible to spin dubbing thin enough to correspond to the bodies of many small spinners. The thinnest body one can make is with simple tying thread in the color corresponding to the spinner's abdomen, and that is the simple method I have adopted in this book.

I am not abandoning my interest and fondness for the soft-hackled fly with this book. In fact, many friends, when told I was working on a book on spinners, frequently asked, "soft-hackled spinners?", to which I had to respond, "no," because the patterns can be tied with either cock or hen hackles and because the patterns are meant to be fished drag free, and not on the swing. However, I have showed many of the first, tied spinners from this book to my wife, Hazel, who, remarked, "they look just like soft hackles."

I have always been interested in the instigations which form inside an individual and make him want to write a book; and it's fascinating to try to trace the steps which have led to that folly. Yes, Hazel may be right. Spinner flies might be, could be, soft- hackled flies, and if they are, it seems only natural that I should continue writing about these wonderful flies in the guise of spinners. Some of you may remember the Rusty Spinner from my last book, SOFT-HACKLED FLY IMITATIONS. That may have been instigator number one. Instigator number two may have been the fact that nobody ever wrote a book on spinners. Instigator number three may have been the fact that I was ignorant of the biology of mayflies and it was high time I learned it. Instigator number four may have been the fact that spinner fishing is a fading art in American fly fishing and this book may help to save it. I'm sure there are others.

It was hinted, and I cant find where, that fly fishing with spinners has a special fascination, a certain nuance, a slight variation in the meaning and the quality of fly fishing. It may be the challenge, itself of trying to duplicate with feather and metal such an exquisite and ethereal thing as a spinner, and the need for delicacy and flawless presentation. Timing of the fishing may be part of the reason. It always seems to happen at the most pleasant part of the day. Maybe it's knowing you're fishing in the adult, sex, death, stage of the insect's life, where the hero-survivors play their last role.

Whatever it is, I've succumbed. Norman Maclean ended his great story with the words, "I am haunted by waters." I'd like to end this introduction with, I am haunted by spinners.

## Acknowledgements

First, of course, I would like to thank my wife, Hazel, who joined me on the majority of our collection trips and who actually wielded the various nets with greater accuracy and aplomb than I. There were times when someone had to test the new spinner patterns on the trout and often, while I was doing that tough job she was still collecting. She helped with the photography and even made suggestions on the writing. I couldn't have finished the book without her help and moral support.

Spinners was not an easy book to layout and I must thank my daughter, Diane Corson, for the beautiful, yet concise design she came up with for this book.

I must thank Dan Gustafson, Ph.D . at Montana State University, here in Bozeman, who identified the spinners for me and who put up with my inane questions. Thanks to him, I didn't have to take entomology 101, 102 and 103, (which I probably would have flunked anyway) to continue this work on spinners and was able to get answers to my perplexing questions immediately when they were fresh in my mind and when they were pertinent to the work at hand. He spent many hours with me and frequently loaned me papers and books from his own vast collection of systematic literature which helped to keep me up to date on the findings of professional workers.

And how do I thank Marvin Nolte, who tied the 30 spinner patterns for me for the formal portraits of them in this book. As many of you know, Marvin is better known for tying full dress salmon flies and has a chapter in Judith Dunham's beautiful book, THE ATLANTIC SALMON FLY, 1991. On top of that, this year, 1995, he won the FFF Buszek fly tying award. Fly tying, I feel, is not an art, except when it comes from Marvin's hands.

I had two good "reads" of the manuscript prior to publication. One was from my good friend, Dean Yannias, who already traveled with me down the bumpy road of self publishing with the same excellent job on SOFT -HACKLED FLY IMITATIONS. The other was from Jesse Lair, who also tested some new spinner patterns with me and who helped with the photography.

I had permission of spring creek owners near Livingston to collect mayflies and try out some new spinner patterns so I must thank Allyn and Agnes O'Hair of

Armstrong Creek, members of the Depuy family and Bob Auger, the river keeper of DePuy spring creek, and Edwin and Helen Nelson of Nelson spring creek. The fly shops in Livingston, Dan Bailey and Montana's Master Angler gave me information about river conditions and hatches, so a thanks to John Bailey and any of his staff who contributed information and Tom Travis and Rick Smith from the Master Angler. And thanks again to the Milesnick family for permission to collect mayflies and try new spinner patterns on their spring creek.

Many other angling friends have made various contributions to the book through suggestions or actually testing various patterns. And a big thanks to all of them.

# Spinner Trek Through The History of Fly Fishing

## Part One

I don't believe I would ever have fly fished or continued to do so after 53 years if there were not the body of literature on the sport which separates it from that practiced by the legendary 'barefoot boy.' One might say the actual physical participation is only secondary to the mental one and I do know some angling bibliophiles who won't even go near a trout stream.

Of course, I'm agreeing with John Waller Hills, who said in A HISTORY OF FLY FISHING FOR TROUT, 1971, "No sport has a finer literature than fishing, and no part of that literature is finer than that devoted to the fly. From the earliest times fishing has never lacked writers who can express themselves; and fly fishing especially has frequently had much more, for authors of outstanding repute have written about it, both in prose and verse."

At least three, modern authors of 'outstanding repute' that I can think of also wrote about fly fishing. They were Hemingway, Traver and Humphrey.

Hills also said in his wonderful history that one of the Dame's famous jury of flies appearing in her TREATISE, 1496, was the red spinner. She didn't call it the red spinner; rather it was a fly to be used "In the beginning of May a good fly, the body roddyd (i.e. ruddy) wool, and lapped about with black silk; the wings of the drake and of the red capons hackle."

Hills compares her dressing to one given by Francis Francis in "A BOOK ON ANGLING," 1867, second edition. "Body, dark red-brown silk, ringed with fine gold thread; legs, a red hackle; tail, three wisps of the same; wing, a dark shiny brown feather, the more brilliant and transparent the better." (The word, red, when applied to hackles, particularly in England, means a shade of brown or reddish brown.)

Hills, back in his own work, continues, "Just consider the two dressings. Red wool dulled by a ribbing of black silk is indistinguishable from red brown silk brightened by gold thread. The basis of the fly, red hackle, is the same in both; the wings are not different. The fly is the same, in detail as well as in substance."

Now, we should let Francis, himself, describe the red spinner, "This is the imago of which the blue dun is the pseudimago, and after its transformation it comes forth a brilliant and much more beautiful insect. Its wings, body, and tail are longer, more slender, and more lustrous, its colour being entirely changed; the body being brown-red, the legs red, and the wings of a bright steely hue. It is a very lively and strong flying insect, and though it occasionally comes on the water in the day-time, yet it more often comes out in the cool of the evening, when it may be seen dancing up and down, rising and falling again in a very peculiar and striking manner in thousands."

That was the insect, now for the imitation. "The body and legs are all pretty plain sailing, but the great difficulty in the fly rests in the wings. There are various feathers used for the wing of this fly, none of which, to my mind, at all accurately represent it, for the wings are so brilliant, sparkling, and transparent, that a mere mass of dull feathers would seem a hopeless imitation indeed...."

Later, "...but the best imitation in feathers, to my mind, is conveyed by the dark shining tips of a blue cock's hackle — those which are grizzled or freckled with a golden tinge at the point, hitting off the resemblance almost exactly, the open fibrous nature of the hackle giving the glassy transparency so much required, and which cannot be conveyed by any other feather, the springiness and play of the cock's hackle being required here also."

We shall hear a similar complaint on the wings of the spinner many times in this chapter.

In his list of flies, Francis also includes THE BROWN SPINNER, the body made of light brown silk, but still ribbed with fine gold wire, and hackled with a lighter colored 'red' (brown) cock's hackle, and lighter shade of feather for the wing. The red spinner, he goes on, should be used on the evening after the blue dun (baetis or blue-winged olive) has been on during the day and the brown spinner after a yellow dun (PMD) has been on during the day.

The red spinner was probably the most famous spinner in the history of fly fishing. Walton pirated it along with the other eleven jury flies from the dame. Cotton, in his contribution to the fifth edition of The Compleat Angler, 1675, listed flies with red-brown dubbing, red silk and "the red Hackle of a Capon over all...." again without names. Besides Francis, the red spinner is found in the fly lists of most major British writers until more modern times when it became the red quill, the difference being a dyed, stripped peacock herl body. A. Courtney Williams sets the fly straight in A DICTIONARY OF TROUT FLIES, Fourth Edition, 1965. "This name (Red Spinner) is loosely applied by anglers to many spinners of the upwinged duns but, correctly speaking, it should be used only for the female spinner of the olive dun. The artificial pattern dates back some hundreds of years and is one of the standard patterns carried by every trout fisherman. Age has done nothing to diminish its popularity and fished wet or dry, there can be no doubt that it is a most useful pattern,..."

Now for the first use of the word, spinner. A DICTIONARY OF FLY-FISHING, by C. B. McCully, 1993, gives the honor to Thomas Best, 1787. It's true, the word is in the book, A CONCISE TREATISE ON THE ART OF ANGLING, but Vernon Gallup has found it in an earlier book, THE ART OF ANGLING by Richard Bowlker, 1746. "The Red Spinner. Comes down the beginning of July, and continues till the middle of the same Month: He is to be Fish'd with only in theEvenings of very hot Days. His Wings are made of a Grey Drake's Feather lightly ting'd with a yellow Gloss: His Body is made of Gold Twist, with a red hackle over it."

Bowlker's Red Spinner, 1829 Edition

After Bowlker's death, his son Charles edited, enlarged and published the book until his death in 1779, after which the book was republished way into the middle of the nineteenth century, a total of some 16 editions.

In the second and subsequent editions, Charles lengthened the season from the middle of June to the end of August. He tells the reader to fish "from seven o'clock as long as you can see," and adds "There are two sorts of Spinners; the one is made with the grey feather of a drake, tinged with a copper-coloured gloss; his body with the red part of the squirrels fur, ribbed with gold twist, and a fine red cock's hackle for the legs; with a long forked tail, made with the harles of a red hackle: The wings of the other Spinner is made with a feather out of the wing of the starling; the body of a dull red mohair, ribbed with gold twist, with a fine red cock's hackle over the body, the tail long and forked, and made as the former. These are both very killing flies, particularly upon rivers: The hook, No. 7 or 8, according to the water you fish in."

Two points made in these dressings tell us the Bowlkers knew the difference between the dun and the spinner: the best time of the year and the day to fish the flies and the inclusion of a long forked tail. They also described the joys of tying, "Even the preparation of the Materials for the artificial fly and the skill and contrivance in making them, and comparing them with the natural, is a very pleasing amusement:..." And they may have also written the first description of dry fly fishing: "The manner of the Fishes taking them, (flies) which is by rising to the surface of the Water, and sometimes out of it...".

The first really good look at a spinner and its dressing in print comes in 1836, when Alfred Ronalds published THE FLY- FISHER'S ENTOMOLOGY. Four duns and their spinner patterns are included, the insect and the imitation of each, colored by hand. The first two are the blue dun and red spinner and the March brown and great red spinner. The dressing of the first is much the same as the Bowlker's, but the illustrations of both the dun and the spinner are nearly as modern as what I can photograph with the best color film and finest macro lenses. There are 10 body segments on a mayfly and the illustrations show 9 of them. The legs and tails of the spinners are much longer than of the duns, as, indeed, they should be.

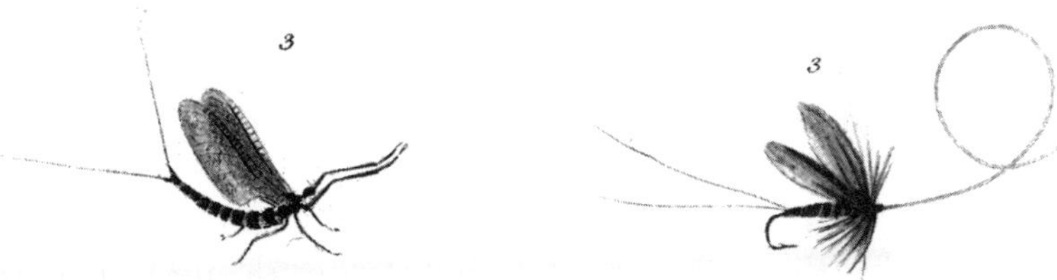


Ronald's Red Spinner, Imago & Red Spinner Imitation

The second two spinner patterns are the jenny spinner, imago of the iron blue dun and the little dark spinner, imago of his turkey brown, (mahogany spinner). Ronalds also describes a small spinner similar in color to the jenny spinner, but whose tail, "increases to quite four times its original length," over the dun. You will find similar treatment of the tails of the new spinner patterns in this book.

Spinner fishing is much closer to dry fly fishing than wet fly fishing. And if we're trying to trace the development of spinners in the history of fly fishing, we should stop at four books of Frederick M. Halford, FLOATING FLIES AND HOW TO DRESS THEM, 1886, DRY-FLY FISHING IN THEORY AND PRACTICE, 1889, DRY FLY ENTOMOLOGY, 1902 and MODERN DEVELOPMENT OF THE DRY FLY, 1910. We also have to visit with Reverand A. E. Eaton without whose work in the classification of Ephemeroptera, prior to these publication dates, Halford's works might not have been written.

I know the reverend through his "A MONOGRAPH ON THE EPHEMERIDAE, published in THE TRANSACTIONS OF THE ENTOMOLOGICAL SOCIETY OF LONDON, 1871, which I found in the Montana State University library. Eaton apologizes for being "obliged to give at second-hand descriptions of many foreign species. These incorporated descriptions I have, for the sake of uniformity, translated into Latin." In preparing for the work, Eaton referred to more than 200 papers and publications, going back to 1634 and written in every major language in Europe. Some reference comes from the US.

Before he gets into the work proper, he deals with fossils of mayflies, "Palaeontologists have adopted a ridiculous course with regard to some insect fossils. Whenever an obscure fragment of a well-reticulate insect's wing is found in a rock, a genus is straightway set up, and the fossil named as a new SPECIES." And, "The following list contains the names of fossils hiterto reputed Ephemeridae upon questionable ground. I shall take no further notice of them."

In the introductory description of the family Ephemeridae, he sounds like the famous TV detective who wanted nothing but the facts. "Antenne aristate; the basal two joints the largest, the bristle many-jointed. Ocelli three. Oculi compound or complex. Legs slender, the anterior pair the longest; tarsi distinctly jointed, terminated by claws."

No fooling around with Eaton. He next describes the copulating flight, egg laying, the nymph, its emergence, and back again to the spinner. "In some genera, the subimago is the permanent aerial state of the female; in most cases, however, the subimaginal pellicle is cast sooner or later, according to the temperature of the air and the habit of the genus. The dingy appearance of the subimago, the comparative shortness of its setae and tarsi, and the ciliate terminal border of the wings, nearly always distinguish it from the imago.

"The composition of the abdomen of Ephemeridae has been the subject of much dispute. Some consider it to be ten-jointed, others reckon nine joints." Eaton goes with ten joints and explains why clearly, although workers still argue the point, today. So, in 165 pages of the Monograph,

Eaton describes "about 178 species of the mayfly, many of them for the first time. In the professional journals, you'll still see his name behind this or that genus or species and know he left an indellible mark on the entomology of the mayfly. But we're still not through with the reverand.

Halford is listed for the first time as a member of the Entomological Society of London in 1893, and cites Eaton in his second book briefly. There is no great show of entomology in the first two books but in DRY-FLY ENTOMOLOGY, Eaton is quoted often and at length on ephemeroptera nymph, dun and spinner. Here is a sample on the spinner mating flight. "A fluttering, swift ascent and then a passive leisurely fall, many times repeated. The body, during the rise, is carried in a position very little out of the perpendicular, with the legs extended upwards in advance, and the setae trailed behind. During the descent the body, less steeply inclined, is steadied by the half-spread motionless wings and the outstretched setae and legs."

Halford, himself, describes a flight of sherry spinners. "...the late Mr. Marryat and I, looking at some of them against the sky took them for a flight of ants." During a later evening they netted some. "They were a revelation to us; each sherry spinner was carrying, held against the hinder end of her abdomen, a little blue-green round ball of eggs, and at the least touch this object was liberated. Their eggs were held in position by the pressure of the three setae, which were doubled under the abdomen and kept up to the thorax.

"The reason of our mistaking the sherry spinners in the air for winged ants was that the setae turned up under the abdomen were of course invisible, and the ball of eggs was suggestive of the form of an ant's body."

There are 90 patterns in FLOATING FLIES, only 6 of which are spinners; Red Quill, Red Spinner, Detatched Red

Spinner, Claret Spinner, Jenny Spinner and Hackle Red Spinner. The last I find the most interesting of all because one of the patterns in this book is tied in the same manner. And Halford pays the Hackle Red Spinner quite a compliment. "Possibly the reason of flies of the red spinner species killing well during the early evening rise is due to the fact that the majority of Ephemerida on the water are in the imago stage. It is possible that the cooling of the air after a hot summer's day kills or weakens them, and it is well known that the hotter the day, as a rule, the better is the evening rise, provided there is no mist. There is another reason, and most likely the best one, for accounting for the great numbers of spinners on the water, in the fact that, having laid their eggs, and thus fulfilled their province of reproduction, their life is at an end, and they fall on the water with their wings flat."

The hand painted flies in the FLOATING FLIES are quite beautiful, and lifelike, but it appears the spinner patterns (except the Hackle Red Spinner) are tied with the wings quite upright just like the duns, not spent as one would expect. But, let's continue. "This flat-winged state in which they appear on the water is to my mind one of the strongest arguments in favour of dressing spinners hackle or buzz fashion. They should have plenty of hackle, although hackle flies float very much better than one would think, but are a little more difficult to see."

In DRY FLY ENTOMOLOGY the total number of patterns grows to 100, fourteen of which are spinners, but with a larger percentage now to be tied hackle style. The bodies of most of these spinners were tied with various natural or dyed quills, horsehair and the refuse ends of silkworm gut. In body design, however, Halford makes an interesting prediction which has certainly come true. "It is, however, quite possible that in the near future quill, gut, and hair for bodies will have been abandoned in favour of dubbing. This statement may give the idea of a retrograde step, seeing that fur and wool were probably the first materials used for the bodies of artificial flies."

It's not until MODERN DEVELOPMENT OF THE DRY FLY that Halford's spinner patterns with wings assume a more natural look. He has reduced the total number of patterns to only 33, 10 of which are duns and 9 of which are spinners. There are no hackle style spinners, instead, wings are made of the tips of various cock hackles "set on horizontally." Here is a typical pattern. "No. 17.—PALE WATERY SPINNER (FEMALE) Wings.—Two cock hackles dyed a full shade of Naples yellow...set on horizontally. HACKLE.—A cock hackle dyed a full shade of Naples yellow...BODY.—Stripped condor dyed a full shade of Naples yellow..WHISK.--Gallina dyed a very pale Naples yellow..."

In all of Halford's books, tying instructions and drawings are excellent, and have not been surpassed to this day. In DRY FLY ENTOMOLOGY, he throws out half hitches and suggests the whip finish. In MODERN DEVELOPMENT OF THE DRY FLY, he recommends a new American, lever-operated vice called Thompson. The drawings are extra large, very visible, the tying thread appearing to be 1/16". Instructions are minimal. For example, to dress spinners with hackle-point wings, the reader is instructed to tie in the cock hackle tips first, followed by the hackle, stem first, "with its point over the head of the fly." Then he ties in the tail and body material, and wraps it up to the wings. The hackle is wound in back of and in front of the wings, tied in and the fly completed with the whip finish. Simple, don't you agree?

From Halford's, MODERN DEVELOPMENT OF THE DRY FLY

What was the reason for the drastic reduction in the number of patterns and how did they perform? Well, 100 patterns from DRY FLY ENTOMOLOGY were just too many to carry and Halford must have been plagued with letters to reduce the number. The large number was also ridiculed by other writers. "My own experience of the exclusive use of the new patterns during the 1904 season was so satisfactory that I am tempted to recapitulate it in tabulated form," wrote Halford. This was on the Itchen. "Out of the total of 306 trout, 146 were taken with duns, 111 with spinners, and two with mayfly, or no less than 259 in all with imitations of the Ephermeridae." These are interesting statistics for the theme of this book, because they show fishing with spinners was almost as important to chalkstream anglers as fishing with duns.

One of Halford's staunchest supporter's was G. E. M. Skues. They could even have been friends at one time because in DRY-FLY ENTOMOLOGY, Skues is given 9 pages to describe how he dresses an upright winged quill-bodied dun, and it was Halford who put up Skues for membership in the Flyfishers' Club. But in 1910, Skues published MINOR TACTICS OF THE CHALK STREAM, the first of four books, all devoted to nymph and wet fly fishing on chalk stream. One would not expect to find much about spinners in a book on wet flies, but Skues was never predictable in his writing. No, indeed. He was sly and funny and would just as soon write doggeral as serious prose on fly fishing. So, it's not surprising to find in his first book, a few pages entitled "OF THE USE OF SPINNERS DURING THE RISE OF DUNS,..." Skues writes of a friend who used nothing but a spinner, the red quill, for a whole season and did as well with the one fly as in other seasons with a larger selection. Skues goes on, "It will also be found that during the rise of any kind of dun its spinner will often take as well as, if not better than, the subimago pattern. For instance, a Red Spinner during a rise of olives, a Claret spinner when the iron-blue is on, and a Sherry spinner when the blue- winged olive is on."

Skues also suggests a spinner first thing in the morning, "And when...before the rise comes on, an odd fish or so may be found in position putting up occasionally at something, spinners may legitimately be suspected. Therefore it may be that, when the rise comes on, the memory of a recent acquaintance with more delicious morsels than the current duns leads to a readiness on his part to absorb the floating imitation spinner."

In the same book, Skues urges the angler to fish spinners... "flush with the water," which is "perilously close to the edge of wet. Tup's Indispensable fished as a spinner in the evening rise will often kill better semi-submerged and flush with the surface than thoroughly dried and oiled."

In THE WAY OF A TROUT WITH A FLY, 1921, his second book, Skues comes perilously close to the edge of today's spinner patterns with his rusty spinner. "From the time when the pale watery dun first puts in an appearance to the end of the season, one of the most useful of chalk-stream patterns for evening use is the Little Rusty Spinner."

The fly is tied with, "hot orange silk dubbed with fine pig's wool or seal's fur of red-ant colour—a deep rich mahogany red—ribbed with fine gold wire and hackled with a rusty dun cock's hackle, sharp and bright, and with whisks of three fibres of a honey-dun cock's shoulder hackle, it proves extraordinarily attractive at the time when small spinners come on the water, and according to my experience it fishes as well slightly submerged as floating. Dressed on No. 1 or even No. 2 hook it is an excellent representation of the male spinner of the blue-winged olive. No angler should be without it at the appropriate season of the year."

We should move on to two more angling writers, J. C. Mottram and John Dunne, whose major concerns in designing spinners were the same as mine...mainly transparency, weight and luminousity. We'll start with Mottram's, FLY-FISHING: SOME NEW ARTS AND MYSTERIES, ND, "He who has closely looked at dun or spinner will be forever convinced that man can never make a complete copy of the insects, but must be content with only caricatures, so delicate in form and modelling, so subtle in colour, so varying in transparency are their parts."

He analyzes transparency: "This quality, that an object may possess, is not a common quality, and even when present is taken little note of, because its demonstration requires a special and unusual lighting. The object must be lit by a bright light from behind. People do not as a rule examine objects against a bright sky, yet this is how a fish must view a floating fly."

He weighs the weight: "Flies built for aerial life are light, and so must the angler's flies be light and buoyant. So highly characteristic is this quality of flies that to copy it must be one of the fly-tier's first aims.

He presents "THE TRANSPARENT JENNY SPIN-

NER.—The jenny spinner,...is chosen to exemplify this type of fly, in which transparency, above all things is imitated. The transparent part of this fly's abdomen is usually made of horsehair or gut, as in Mr. Halford's pattern, but, as is shown in Fig. 2, which is a view against the sky, it does not do its duty. To my mind, one of the best ways of indicating transparency is to omit the transparent parts altogether." Figure two shows the artificial fly as Halford tied it, which, by the way, would be the view presented by 99% of today's dubbed body spinner patterns. Then, he gives the dressing for the transparent Jenny Spinner: "Tail, three long white cock hackle barbs: abdomen, a few turns of red brown floss silk near the bend of the hook—the rest of the hook as far as the thorax is left uncovered; thorax, red brown floss silk; wings, white cock hackle—four or five turns are made round the hook, afterwards the hackle is cut, leaving only those fibres which project laterally, these will rest flat on the water and keep the fly afloat in a most natural manner; floating hackle, none is used."

Mottram has a drawing of this fly looking at it from underneath, and I must say it looks like a good imitation and one well worth trying and easy to make.

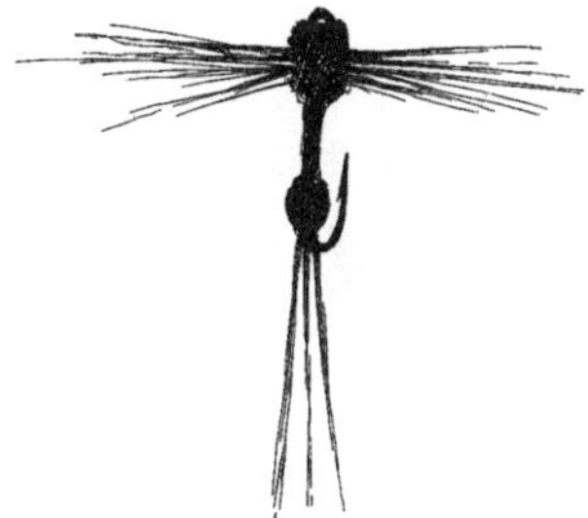

FIG. 3.

Mottram's, Transparent Jenny Spinner

John Dunne's flies, on the other hand, are not easy to make. In fact, they're impossible to make now, 70 years af ter the publication of his book, SUNSHINE AND THE DRY FLY, 1924. We can incorporate some of his ideas, but we can never make his flies because he used formulas which today have no meaning whatsoever. Here, for example is No. 12. Olive Spinner (Female).

Hook: No. 1.
Body: 2(298) x 1/2(287).
Tying silk: M. 6.
Ribbing: M. ll.
Hackle: Seven turns of E.
Whisks: Pale honey."

Well, what are these things? Body material, for example is two strands of an imitation silk from plait No. 298 blended with 1/2 of a strand of the same material from plait No. 287. One buys these strands, together with the tying silk, ribbing and hackles from Messeena and Co., 94, Upper Clapton Road, London, E. 5., if one intends to tie the flies, or one buys the flies made up from Hardy who sold them through its stores and catalogs for many years until at least 1966, according to one of the Hardy catalogs I own.

There were other instructions in the book which do have meaning. The hook had to be painted white in order to hide the shank in the transparent covering. Hackles on duns were clipped on the bottom in a narrow angled, inverted V, and in a wide angled V, top and bottom on the spinner patterns.

FIG. 9.
Dunne's Method of clipping duns and spinners

And the fly was coated with 'Sunshine oil' which is a, "thickish, colourless paraffin sold by chemists for medicinal purposes." (Supposedly, the body glowed when coated with the oil.)

It must be admitted, there were some good ideas in SUNSHINE AND THE DRY FLY. The patterns were around for a long time, indicating they were effective. Dunne's approach to transparency and luminousity in duns and spinners was different and well thought out. But, alas, Meseena and Co are no more and neither are the silk manufacturers who, "would be bound to see to it that the relationship between these tints and numbers remained unaltered;..."

Poor Mr. Dunne. Perhaps he thought his 1924 world of fly fishing and fly tying was going to last forever.

## Part Two

We're going to start the second part, the American part, of the spinner trek with Theodore Gordon, who wrote for the English journal, Fishing Gazette, from the late nineteenth century until his death in the early part of the current century, and who corresponded with many English authors. "Few fly fishermen today are directly familiar with his work," said John McDonald in THE COMPLETE FLY FISHERMAN, 1947. Fewer still would even remember the name, Gordon, if it hadn't been for McDonald's admirable work on the man's "rare dedication to the sport."

But let's listen to Gordon and wonder how he became so knowledgeable on spinners at such an early stage in American fly fishing. "In the former state" meaning the dun state, "the colors are quite dull and the wings opaque. As soon as their wings gain strength the insect flies to the shore and hides among the bushes. After remaining in this condition for some days, it sheds its whole covering, coming out in bright colors and with clear, glassy, sparkling wings. These wings, by the way, cannot be well imitated, and the best thing to do is to dress the fly hackles only. (A hackle with dark center and golden edge answers for wings and legs.)" I must break in here and say a similar hackle is the favorite for spinner patterns in this book.

"As duns and spinners these flies do not feed at all, their only duty in this latter state being to perpetuate their species. The males may be seen dancing up and down in the air, usually in the evening. They are then on the watch for the females, which are quickly caught when they leave the bushes in which they have sought shelter. The nuptial rites take place in the air and soon after the females deposit their eggs upon the water. Their existence terminates soon after, as both male and female are reduced to mere shells. The little egg quickly sinks to the bottom, on which it finds a lodgment among stone and gravel. In a few weeks it becomes a larvae, to follow its destiny as described."

I think Mr. Gordon meant the plural, eggs, but what about this observation on peacock quills, "The peacock quill certainly makes a very natural-looking ribbed body for many flies, and I should be glad to have it in all colours. It is weak, but by brushing a little varnish or glue in the foundation the body of the fly will endure more hard service." And later on the subject, "The quill-bodied flies absorb but little moisture, are easier to dry, and need not be so full in the hackle."

How about this for common sense and humour. "A well-made artificial fly having a natural appearance and having good colours put into it may answer for more than one species.

"Dun, for instance, is a common colour among insects, from grey to almost purple, a dark blue dun. Yellow is another standard colour, from a pale fleshy yellow through delicate primrose to orange. Brown is quite fashionable, particularly for evening wear, although in spring it is quite proper in the morning, and may run from a soft yellowish brown to brown-red."

Here are nice lessons in egg laying. "Hackle flies may be made to float and kill well. I have used what are called spent spinners a great deal, and these are supposed to represent the day flies in the very last stage of existence, but mine are not always spent. Some insects carry their eggs in a bag at their hinder ends, and when this is conspicuous it must be quite attractive to the trout. The insect may deposit its eggs in one parcel by a single dip in the water, but then again it may not. I have seen them come down from a height, make one dip and fly away, but many flies dip a number of times in one place, then fly a short distance and do it again. I have seen an insect come out from a bush and pound up and down like a piece of machinery, then fly back to the bush."

In a letter to Skues, Gordon uses practically the same words I used to describe the bodies of some spinners. "...This morning I got specimens of dark red spinners, Jenny spinners, most perfect blue duns (the tints of body and wings were exquisite). A peculiar yellowish spinner with brown markings, lace wings and long tail. The strangest fly of all was a big brown spinner, very stout, body looked as if it had been plated and varnished. Wings crinkled glass." Now, look up my gold-plaited spinner in the chapter on Baetis.

Vincent C. Marinaro, I feel, is the first or second most influential writer on fly fishing in the United States. His two books, A MODERN DRY FLY CODE, 1950, and IN THE RING OF THE RISE, 1976, are inspirations to me and are the most parrallel to SPINNERS of any American books I can find. Oh, we don't agree on everything and some of his terrestrial patterns are now obsolete because the insects on which they were based, have disappeared from certain trout areas. But liking fly fishing writers means you can quote much of what they wrote without needing to say it yourself. And very often they say it better.

For example, one of the reasons I wrote SPINNERS is that I feel fly fishing with spinners is slipping away from the American angler. It may already be on its way to obscurity, like Dunne's Sunshine flies. So I needed someone with far more authority than mine to alert the angler reader, and here it is from IN THE RING OF THE RISE. "...American fly-fishermen have long denied themselves the pleasure and satisfaction of fishing to the frenzied rises during a heavy fall of spinners...

"There seems to be some notion that trout do not eat spinners and are, therefore not worth imitating. Certainly the British never made this mistake. In the books of Halford, J. W. Dunne and numerous others, including modern British authors, the spinner is just as highly esteemed as the dun in fishing practice. And the idea that a spinner is not worth eating is erroneous. The dying or dead spinner, even though devoid of eggs and the consequent loss of fats, is nevertheless good eating because the remaining chitinous structure is solid protein material."

Marinaro liked seal's fur for the bodies of his spinners, fashioned after Rube Cross who made a 'chenille' of the seal's fur with well waxed thread doubled and twisted together. To study live and dead spinners, Marinaro built a 'slant' tank where he noticed, "the wings took on a brilliant translucent aspect with long, clear, colorless streaks that are not apparent in an air view of the spinner....I discovered that this effect was created by the folds in the wing acting as water traps to form light condensers that gathered light above the surface and transmitted this intensified light to the trout."

Now for the Marinaro wings. "A successful spinner wing must gather and condense the light exactly as is done by the natural spinner. This cannot be done with hackle points, fish scales, cellophane, or the body feathers of various birds. This can be done only with hackle fiber wings. Marinaro admits he didn't know who was the first to use hackle fiber for wings, but I would bet he saw a copy of MODERN TROUT FLY DRESSING by Roger Woolley, first published in 1932 in Britain.

In the chapter on spinners, Woolley says, "It is usual now to dress spinners either with spent wings of bright glassy hackle fibres, or as a hackle fly only, ...

"In tying spent spinners with hackle fibre wings the hackle for legs may be dispensed with if desired, the stiff fibres forming the wings being sufficient to float the fly."

Marinaro again with the same meaning, "No support hackle for the spinner is used in the usual sense because the outspread fiber wings provide that support without obscuring the body."

I'm saving both writers' instructions on tying the hackle fibre spinner wing for the section on tying the spinner patterns in this book.

But let's continue with Marinaro on designing and tying spinner patterns. "In reality the spinner is not a dry fly at all but a damp fly, as Col. Harding puts it, something which is halfway between a dry fly and a wet fly. In tying the spinner we are confronted by vast difficulties which make the tying of a dun seem comparatively easy."

An alert again: "It is the oddest thing that in all American angling literature so little has been done to establish a better understanding of fishing to spinners. A beginner would find it almost impossible to locate a satisfactory presentation of precept and example for his guidance."

Remember what Skues said about fishing spinners first thing in the morning. Marinaro says it too, "It is sometimes profitable to use the spent artificial on the following morning, for the spent forms may remain along the edges of the stream, where they have been caught or trapped by twigs, leaves or the bank itself."

Let me add that I think there is an accumulative effect to any kind of spinner activity, which can happen anytime and which can be noticed considerably later and much further downstream from its source or beginning. The angler sees no spinners flying around him, yet if he gets down and looks closely at the stream's surface, he will see countless numbers of spinners floating by flush with the surface. If he picks one up he will think it dead, it has so little rigid, positive form. Closer examination, however, usually shows some slim sign of life, a leg or abdomen moving ever so slightly. In this form, think how easily and lazily the spinner is taken by a trout. Think how many times you saw a trout rise when there were no duns or caddis or stone flies or midges or anything flying around or on the water. The trout was not feeding on air or amusing itself. It was dining on spinners.

## Part Three: The Hatch Books

The first 'hatch' book in American fly fishing, of course, was MATCHING THE HATCH, by Ernest G. Schwiebert, Jr. It was first published in 1955 and went through eight printings by 1972. I don't think the book ever really went out of print and I have heard (1995) that the author is coming out with a new version of the book.

Like the books which followed it, MATCHING THE HATCH gives priority to the duns, although the definitions of many spinners and their imitations are included in the plates, although they are all with upright wings. In "Hatching charts and fly patterns," the author listed 28 dry fly spinner patterns and 15 wet fly spinner patterns, which shows there was still some interest in wet fly fishing back there in the fifties.

Other 'hatch' books followed, creating an excellent body of literature in the U.S. pertaining to the emergence of duns: SELECTIVE TROUT, 1971, by Doug Swisher and Carl Richards; HATCHES, 1975, by Al Caucci and Bob Nastasi; MEETING AND FISHING THE HATCHES, 1977, by Charles R. Meck; MAYFLIES, THE ANGLER, AND THE TROUT, 1980, by Fred L. Arbonna, Jr.; and THE COMPLETE BOOK OF WESTERN HATCHES 1981, by Rick Haefle and Dave Hughes. These are all difficult works matching professional, entomological skills with angling and writing skills and proclivities, a rare combination. All of these books are monumental endeavors. None of them could have been done in less than three years and none of them could have been researched without cameras, microscopes and laboratory equipment and cars and money and the least important of all...time.

Most of the fly fishing in America today is based on one or more of these books; their research, fly patterns, and tying and angling methods. In this little history of spinners, we shall look briefly at the tying methods chosen by the various authors and in the order of the book's appearance.

Swisher and Richards have more than one type of spinner, two of which are no-hackle up to size 10. Wings on the no-hackles are made from hen hackle feather tips and from partridge breast feathers tied spent or half spent. The authors also give one hackle pattern which can represent spinners with wings upright, intermediate and full spent wing positions. Bodies are made from various dubbings. Tails come from cock hackles, which are tied over a clump on the rear of the hook and widely spread.

In TYING THE SWISHER/RICHARDS FLIES, 1980, a pamphlet, the authors list the No-Wing Spinner, which is "used in situations where the hyaline wings of the spinner are all but invisible to the trout." Do we see a little history repeating itself here?

The Caucci and Nastasi spinners have similar wide-spread tails, a dubbed body and a cock hackle tied in the vicinity of the thorax, with dubbing in front of the hackle. "We recommend trimming patterns to semi-spent, as they can always be trimmed to flush floating, fully-spent versions which are more easily seen in riffles of pocket water."

"For spent wings of the spinner, I like white or very pale gray polypropylene tied perpendicular and flat," writes Charles Meck. He also suggests a cock hackle wound in front of and behind the wing. For bodies he recommends spun fur and stripped hackle stems and stripped peacock quills, dyed and natural, which, as we have seen, follows some of the British turn of the century styles.

Arbonna lets Mike Lawson do the tying for him in his book, MAYFLIES, THE ANGLER, AND THE TROUT. Dubbed bodies and wings of either polypropolene or hen hackle tips are recommended. Tails are made from stiff hackle fibers which are pulled up and fanned out by the tying thread.

The WESTERN HATCHES authors, Rick Hafele and Dave Hughes, rely on the spinner patterns of several other writers including Swisher and Richards, Polly Rosborough, Caucci and Nastasi, Ernest Schweibert and others.

# The Final Molt

The adult, winged mayfly is born twice...once when it emerges from the nymphal skin and is known as the dun and again when it emerges from the dun skin and is known as the spinner. The time between the two 'births' varies from a few minutes to a few days.

There is considerable conjecture about the reason for the two winged stages because the mayfly is the only insect which does this. One reason given by workers, (the rather chummy name used in the scientific journals to identify professional entomologists) is that it would be impossible for spinners to grow such long and reversible fore legs (longer in the males) and tails in a single molt, as in the first from nymph to dun. And we shall see the importance of the great length of the legs and tails as we go along.

The description of the emergence of the dun has been well covered in the 'hatch' books so we don't have to travel that road again. The final molt to spinner, however, has not received much attention except in scientific publications. Once the dun emerges, it can take flight anytime. The length of the ride on the water, workers say, depends on the time it takes for the wings to dry and for the flight muscles to warm up to operating temperature. Eventually the dun lifts off the water rather heavily, and in a labored flight gains some altitude and flies in a fairly, straight line to the bank. (I have watched some duns skid across the water to the bank or some other kind of vegetation and get themselves away from the water in that manner.) Once on shore, the dun seeks protective shelter in the leaves of a tree or blades of grass where it will rest and 'ripen'. Anglers some times confuse the flight of the dun with that of the spinner but spinner flights, attracting mates or laying eggs, will last much longer and are far more acrobatic.

Final molting depends on many factors of which temperature, humidity and light are the most important. In laboratories, or in other artificial habitats like my home, the duns probably molt faster than they would outside where autumn temperatures can drop to below freezing soon after nightfall. I wondered how Baetis duns could survive these late season night time temperatures and asked Gustafson how they do it. He simply said, they don't, they die.

Duns waiting to molt are quiescent and will remain so for hours at a time with their wings in the classic, upright position. They have a pretty good hold on to whatever surface they're on and this may be necessary for the molt to be successful. One of the first signs that the molt is beginning is the lowering of the wings to the spent position. Next, they are angled back quite severely as on a delta winged aircraft. Now the top of the thorax or mesonotum is fully exposed, and it looks like one of those shiny, wrinkled foreheads on Star Trek. Something seems to be stirring inside the insect. Quite suddenly a crack appears lengthwise in the wrinkled exuvia and the same, identical wrinkling can be seen through it. Now, things start to happen quickly. A new head of the insect appears in the crack, the dun having pulled it back and up through it. The head and longer front legs (up to twice the length of the previous dun legs on the male) and body start to slide forward pulling new wings out of the old. If the insect has trouble getting the rest of himself out, it bends its head, thorax and body back and forth pulling forward with its exposed legs (like someone trying to remove a stubborn cork from a wine bottle) until all of him or her including the much longer tails are free of the exuvia or shuck. The instinct of the dun to become a spinner seems to me to be very strong as if it knows this is not the last nor best part of its life.

The exuvia on the wings is not substantial enough to retain its shape and collapses, while all the other body parts including the legs, (still holding on to the surface) body segments, male claspers and tails are perfectly maintained giving us a sort of clear, plastic replica of the former insect. The molt can happen with the insect in any position; upside down, hanging perpendicular or rightside up on a level plane. I have also noticed that duns with imperfect, unfurled wings cannot molt successfully, but become trapped in the wing exuviae and spin hopelessly until they are exhausted and die. It's quite possible this is how this stage of the mayfly got its name.

It should be added here that not all mayflies molt in a fixed or stationary position. Some angling writers believe species of Tricorythodes molt in mid air although I have seen many of them molt on the ground, on vegetation and on the body and windows of my car, where they seem to go through the same molting process described here. I would not argue too strongly against the mid air molting because I have seen shucks raining down from trico swarms and have netted trico spinners with shucks still hanging from them. Another species, Epheron album, does not run true to form. In it, the three-tailed female breeds as a dun while the two-tailed male molts to spinner in mid-air because his middle and hind legs are so weak and reduced he can never land on anything solid. And there is a rare species which sheds all of the subimaginal pellicle from its body, legs and tails only... but not from its wings.

There is a kind of sleight of hand in the molt. Your eyes are glued to the insect. You don't want to miss anything. Yet, when it's over, you're not sure you saw what you saw. It's also hard to believe that the spinner and the dun are the same insect. The dun is lackluster, thick and stodgy with dull, hairy wings of little translucency. The spinner is sparkling and jewel-like, and smooth and luminous with bright, clear wings of maximum transparency. One worker suggested the discarding of all that hair in the outer cuticle "lightens the body weight for flying," and, "favors flying by diminishing friction against the air."

## The Mating

The mating flight is composed of recently transformed male adults and can take place over the water, over the bank or even inland quite a distance. Some species have a penchant for tarred roads and parking lots, particularly when they are lined with trees. The swarm is usually not too high, although I have seen trico swarms a hundred feet in the air. Where a river runs through a canyon, male spinners will sometimes fly at the rim even though the river may be hundreds of feet below.

You can expect to see mating flights at anytime during the fishing season. In fact, you should expect to see them whenever you see duns, because every dun, male and female, which molts successfully will return to the river area as a spinner. In the earlier part of the season mating flights are more likely to occur in the mid or late afternoon, but as the year progresses, the flights will show earlier and later. The best way to observe a flight is against the sun. There can be as few as a dozen males in the flight or hundreds, except in trico swarms where there can be hundreds of thousands of males and females. The most distinguishing feature of the flight is an up and down rhythm or dance which no other insect seems to have. Up and down distances vary from specie to specie, but an average might seem to be from up to ten feet high and down to two feet above the ground or water. All of the downward movements are in an energy- saving glide, the wings glistening in the sun as the male strives to get the greatest amount of free drift. Tails are held almost perpendicular and move back and forth like rudders during the glide downward, illustrating the importance of their longer length. At the bottom position of the fall, the male beats his wings rapidly and climbs back up to the top position before gliding back down again. This is a demonstration of real flying power and skill and can continue for hours in the same spot, or until a female of the species interrupts the cycle.

She appears from nowhere, flies straight into the swarm and selects a mate. They are joined immediately in mid air and fly together like an old biplane in a rather slow, straight, low angling line towards the ground. During the flight, the male grasps the female from beneath by curving the long, reversible fore legs back over her thorax and using his clasper at the base of the tails to grasp her abdomen. He bends his abdomen upwards and she bends hers downward. Copulation starts and ends while the pair slowly descends to the ground. (Mating could also occur over water, in which case the pair must fly to the bank or something solid to "uncouple" themselves after copulating. See the chapter on the Gray Drake, Siphlonurus occidentalis.)

Egg Laying

With the eggs in her body cavity now fertilized the female spinner develops a u-shaped curve at the 7th or 8th segment of her abdomen, where in a very short time a ball of eggs will appear. The dominant color is a shade of green, although on PMD female spinners the ball is a luminous blue green. Workers say the bigger the female, the more eggs she will lay. A trico for example could have up to 1200, while a green drake could have up to 8000. And larger specimens in a given species will have more eggs than their smaller partners.

The egg ball is quite visible on hovering female spinners, and must represent a large percentage of the insect's total weight. She cannot hold up her hind end and flies with her body almost perpendicular, looking for the right place on the water to get rid of her burden. I netted many PMD egg- carrying spinners with the intention of photographing them and the egg balls. My camera was set up on a level bank a few feet from the stream. Everytime I caught one in the net, I would hurry to the camera, but invariably, by the time I got there, she would have let the ball of eggs go and it would be rolling around in the bottom of the net. The ball is round and hard and can actually be picked up with a pair of tweezers.

Actual egg-laying methods vary from species to species. The one I became the most familiar with was the PMD. This was on a shallow riffle on a spring creek not too far from my home which I visited frequently during July and August of '93 and '94. All kinds of mating activity occurred there, mostly in the late afternoon and early evening. Duns liked to leave the water here. Male spinners swarmed and paired off with females. And female spinners, heavy with eggs, returned to the spot to deposit their eggs. It was a real cornucopia of mayfly activity and I was very fortunate to find it. Sometimes everything seemed to be happening at once. The spot was at a sharp bend in the creek and right in the bend was a large, bushy kind of tree, at the base of which was a shallow, choppy riffle. There were not many such identifying land marks along the creek and perhaps the mayflies, particularly those females ready to lay eggs, used it for the same purpose. Like, "if you just fly upstream a little way, you'll find a large, bushy tree and there underneath it is a riffle tailormade for egg laying."

Egg carrying PMD's are perhaps the most violent egg layers in the mayfly kingdom. I saw many approach the riffle, fly down to within two feet of the choppy surface and just throw themselves into the creek like dive bombers. I would continue to look down the current to try to pick out the insect floating on the surface, but only rarely did I see one moving away. I thought it was also possible that if one bombing didn't release the eggs, the spinner might fly back off the water and try it again.

Females are supposed to fly upstream to lay their eggs to compensate for the downstream drifting of eggs and hatching nymphs. If the PMD's did this, I thought I would walk downstream, try to pick up one in flight and follow her back up to the big, bushy tree. I walked a half mile on the creek, but never found a spinner moving upstream.

There are at least four egg-laying methods recorded in workers' journals; dropped in a string from a couple of feet over the water with the female then dropping to the water and squeezing out the remaining eggs in a death struggle; laid underwater with the female crawling down a stone, or weed or some other submerged limb or vegetation; released in batches by striking the water with the tip of her abdomen and washing off a few eggs at each encounter; and dropped as a ball from a height of several feet in a manuever suggestive of dive-bombing, in which the bushy tree PMD's may be included except they went in with the eggs.

# Spinners and their Imitations

Spinners are arranged alphabetically in this section, first by genus or subgenus, then by species in that genus, followed by anglers' names. The information; size, color, dates, flying and mating habits, egg laying, is based on the actual capture and observation of the insect either in the dun or in the spinner stage. More often, the capture occurred in the dun stage, the insect then observed during the period when it changed to a spinner. In the few instances, adult mayflies were borrowed from the collection of Dan Gustafson. The idea and early planning for the book occurred in the fall of 1992, with collecting and identifying beginning in 1993 (a high water year) and continuing through 1994 and 1995.

Coverage includes many of the famous rivers and private and public spring creeks in Montana, Yellowstone National Park, and one river in Idaho, the Henry's Fork. Some eastern spinners are also included. Information gained by the reader surely can be applied to his own streams and water conditions.

I am not interested in telling the reader where to fish in these areas and very often the exact location of a particular spinner 'find' or activity will remain anonymous. The purpose of this section of the book and the whole book is to describe the spinner species as closely as possible, kind of water in or on which the insect was found, time of day and year and to suggest the size, form and color of an imitation together with any fishing hints I can offer the reader. The dominant color of the body of the spinner will be matched to the corresponding Danville thread, and gold or other colored ribbing. If you prefer the stripped quill bodies, you will use similarly dyed or marker-colored quills.

Published systematic literature on various spinners will also be quoted whenever deemed necessary or helpful. I am indebted to Dan Gustafson for the use of his collection of these invaluable reports and the help he has given me in learning to understand them.

# Baetis tricaudatus

It's easy to love a Baetis. It is the first mayfly we see on our favorite river in the spring and the last we see before we hang up the rod in October or November. Because it comes so early and so late, it is subjected to the worst kind of weather and we fish it in snow, sleet and rain often accompanied by wind.

Low clouds. No sun. A soft dampness in the air. That's Baetis weather. Freezing temperatures kill many duns before they molt into spinners and mate, yet the sufficient few tolerate whatever mother nature throws at them. They hide low in the weeds near the river bank, perhaps moving to the lee side when the wind is raging and to the warm, lit side when the sun is showing. The survivors could molt in 24 hours. Some duns I planted on DePuy and Armstrong in October, 1994, survived for five days!

You all know Baetis. It's the 'blue dun' of the romantic fly fishing past, or the blue-winged olive to Easterners, or simply the 'olive', large and small or dark and light, to the British. It is a small mayfly, as small as 1/8", with an olive body and smoky, gray blue wings, which always look too big for the body and which can cause the angler to throw a fly at a fish that's two sizes too large. There are two tails and every species has hind wings which are difficult to see. (The Pseudocloeon and Cloeon genera, also of the Baetidae, have no hind wings.) Males, as duns and as spinners, have large, flattish caramel colored eyes which look like they're going to shoot right out of the insect's head. The eyes remind me of the caps bellboys used to wear.

As spinners, Baetis tricaudatus male bodies turn light brown with the middle segments going almost clear or hyaline. The female is single colored in a yellowish brown, more like gold, brighter and duller from one girl to the next. The wings, of course, are hyaline and there are two tails.

I have found it difficult trying to describe the colors of the bodies of spinners. Here might be a good explanation from AN ANGLER'S ENTOMOLOGY, J. R. Harris, 1970. "The translucency of the abdomens of duns and spinners greatly increases the difficulty of describing their colours. This quality is most apparent in male spinners, and an examination of the first six or seven segments shows that this portion of the abdomen contains little more than the air-inflated digestive tract, and that most of the colour and opacity is confined to the integument. The last three or four segments are more opaque, as they contain the internal male genital organs.

"The abdomen of a female spinner is completely filled with eggs in the first eight segments, and is, therefore, opaque before the eggs have been passed, but it becomes translucent after the spinner has oviposited."

Baetis is big and widespread. There are more than 60 species. The family Baetidae, to which the Baetis belongs, "is found on all continents and on many islands. It is absent from New Zealand, although its closest relative, Siphlaenigma, occurs there. At extremely high northern latitudes and in high altitude streams of North America and Asia, Baetis is the only mayfly genus present." MAYFLIES OF NORTH AND CENTRAL AMERICA, EDMUNDS, JENSEN AND BERNER, 1976.

And Baetis is also one of the first-known mayfly genera, having been described by a worker named Leach in 1815.

In Montana and other northwestern states, B. tricaudatus is necessarily multi-brooded, with at least two generations per year. On Armstrong spring creek, I have netted duns as early as February 27 and as late as December 15. The same mayfly appears on the Madison in Yellowstone Park in late October. The rise of the early Baetis on the spring creeks near Livingston is spasmodic, beginning around 11 a.m. and lasting for two or three hours. If the wind is not blowing, fishing can be quite good, the trout lined up in their favorite places and taking the first duns of the year with relish. The wind makes the fishing more difficult and more interesting, knocking down many of the duns and driving them to one bank or the other, (usually the east bank), the trout following the wind to where the duns are.

Since I started SPINNERS in the spring of '93, I've watched many trout feed without a fly rod in my hand. This is painful, (someone's got to do the dirty work) but enlightening because the perspective and objective are different. Guides know what I'm talking about. I'm also in direct competition with the trout in front of me for the insects coming down and I certainly learned more about the way trout feed on Baetis duns with only a bug net in my hand. On the spring creeks during windy days, for example, I noticed that the head and shoulders of a trout are well out of the water when he takes a dun. On the same water later in mid summer, he rises hardly at all, showing very little of himself preferring to just sip the insect in. An explanation may well be he knows the wind could blow the dun away at the last moment causing him to go through all that trouble for nothing, if he were not up and ready.

I also noticed that once the trout has selected his feeding position, he does not change it very much, relying on the hand of providence to send him breakfast, lunch and dinner at his chosen eating table. He will not veer too far to the right or left to intercept an insect. You can see him measuring distances in his head, "there goes a nice, fresh dun over on my right. He's more than two feet away, though. If I go after him, I might miss one coming right over my head." At times, he can't make up his mind. He'll start over to the right or left after a dun, then stop and return to the table.

Then there is the smart trout who eliminates one whole side to watch by setting table right on the edge of a bank or island or weed bed. His looking is in just two directions (not three); up and to the right or left. My biggest non-migratory rainbow was one of these guys on the Henry's Fork on June 18, 1993. He was one of those 26 to 30 inchers washed over the Island Park dam by accident a short time before. Fish like him seem to know the angler cannot achieve a drag free float near his table, so any dragging mayfly he leaves alone. Simple. He left alone a rusty spinner and a green drake, but a dragging Mothers Day Caddis from SOFT-HACKLED FLY IMITATIONS was ok and he took it and was landed without even going into my backing.

At times, the imitation of a different order of insects than what the trout is eating at his table, produces satisfactory results. You're tempted to stay with the Baetis because that's what's on the water and that's what the trout are eating by the hundreds. Charlie Loveless, Bozeman fly tyer and occasional guide, designed a small, floating caddis made with a brown and grizzly hackle, tying thread body and short coastal deer hair for wings, which he says works quite well during the difficult rise of Baetis. He may or may not trim the bottom part of the wound hackle depending on how effective it is when he first throws it at rising trout. If it works as is, ok. If it doesn't, he trims the bottom portion of the hackle at streamside which makes the fly sit lower in the film, and which, when required, makes the fly more effective. But fishing spinners (what this book is about, remember) before or after the rise of Baetis duns late or early in the fishing year should be as effective as a fly of a different order. Nature's law is if there are duns, there will be spinners. It's just that from October to March many of the duns are not going to make it to the spinner stage. How few? Let's turn to John W. Hill's book, RIVER KEEPER, 1934, for a possible clue. At the end of this fine work, is an appendix which is the recording of the kind of fly found on the Houghton Fishing Club Test water in England from October 12, 1917, to April 6, 1918, a total of 81 days. Spent fly, spinners that is, was recorded on 29 occasions, the fewest during December and February and the most during March.

The issue of what happens to spinners during the colder months was also taken up by J. C. Mottram in THOUGHTS ON ANGLING, (ND), which I also quoted in SOFT-HACKLED FLY IMITATIONS. "THE CHANGE FROM DUN TO SPINNER.—In March, and especially in April, millions of duns hatch out, yet it is rare to see any spinners dancing until the middle of May or until some really warm weather occurs. What happens to all these millions of duns? Do they die? Do they change to spinners and then die? Do they survive until the hot weather comes?

"I have captured April duns and kept them in jars with foliage; they take a week or more to turn to spinners; they subsequently live about a week and then die. Confinement in a jar is of course very different to natural conditions; perhaps in Nature they do survive until warm weather comes..."

Earlier I mentioned I had planted some tricaudatus

duns on Armstrong and DePuy to see what might happen to them during the warm and cold October days and nights ahead, when overnight low temperatures can go well below freezing. A group of 8 or 10 was collected during the hatch between two and three p.m. from DePuy and from Armstrong, then each placed in a small, screened box with some grass in it. The screened box was then placed in some weeds off the path. That was on Monday, October 17, 1994. As a check, I also brought several duns home in a similar box and put them in my office, where most of them molted in 24 hours.

I examined the duns on the spring creeks every day until Friday, October 21 and found them alive but not molted. The DePuy group looked like any other Baetis duns, but I thought I might photograph them and let them fly away to freedom. The Armstrong group I left in the box with the lid off so they might also escape if they turned into spinners. These went unattended until October 25, when I checked the box and found that all had left the box except one which died as a dun.

But, what temperatures did the tricaudatus tolerate? The Livingston Enterprise daily newspaper gave me the highs and lows.

| | High | Low |
|---|---|---|
| Monday | 45 | 33 |
| Tuesday | 42 | 40 |
| Wednsday | 57 | 30 |
| Thursday | 53 | 47 |
| Friday | 44 | 40 |

Only one night below freezing and not by much, but we know it was a week of rain and sleet and generally inclement weather. From the "experiment" we can perhaps surmise the following:

1. We cannot predict molting times of late and early Baetis duns.

2. They can live for five days or longer in nature if the temperature doesn't go below 30.

3. The relative temperature constancy of a stream makes it easier to predict dun emergence than spinner molting. "Cold weather favors the duns, but makes it risky for spinners." Dan Gustafson.

4. There is much greater opportunity to fish duns than spinners.

5. A large percentage of duns are killed by freezing temperatures, but subsequent hatches of late and early Baetis continue generation after generation and year after year.

One of the first spinner mating dances I witnessed for this book was of Baetis tricaudatus, May 19, 1993. This was on the Madison between Hebgen and Quake lakes, where ice still covered the western ends. It was late in the afternoon, a warm, sunny day. I first saw them 20 or 30 yards from the river in a clearing in the large pines. Light from the sun slanted down on the spinners as if in a cathedral. Perhaps 30 male spinners rose and fell ten feet to two feet over and over again. Strong, rapid wing beats to go up and long, gliding slides with no wing beats to go down. The long tails were held nearly perpendicular, moving from side to side like rudders or ailerons steering each spinner in its downward journey. Every now and then there was a "straight" flyer, a female that seemed to come from nowhere. She flew straight into the group and grasped one of them. Together they left the pack in a long straight angling line and disappeared in the vegetation.

I have not seen female Baetis laying eggs which is supposed to be different from all other mayflies. Where most species deposit fertilized eggs on the surface in one way or another, Baetis females crawl down anything available in the river, vegetation, wooden posts, stones and (even anglers) and lay their eggs in rows. She may die next to the eggs or float back to the surface in the usual spread wing, spent position.

I think there should be three spinner patterns for Baetis species, two conventional ones made like most of the patterns in this book and another I would like to call Syl's Gold Plated Spinner.™

The first:
Hook: Tiemco 100, 16 or 18.
Body: Unithread rusty brown,
ribbed with fine gold wire,
and coated with fly tying cement.
Thorax: Reddish brown.
Wing: Rusty edge or reddish ginger.
Tail: Wood duck flank barbs.

The second:
Syl's Gold Plated Spinner™
Hook: Tiemco 100, 16 or 18.
Body: Danville yellow, plated with thin,
gold wire. Come up the hook
with the thread, then the wire in
close, solid wraps.
Coat with fly tying cement.
Wing: Rusty edge or reddish ginger, divided
and flattened evenly with thumbs and forefingers.
Tail: Two or three barbs from golden pheasant
rooster topping feather.
The third:

The third:

Hook: Tiemco 100, 16 or 18.
Body: Danville yellow, ribbed with thin gold wire.
Hackle: Rusty or ginger.
Thorax: Pinky tan
Tail: Three wood duck flank barbs.

# Caenis

I have a solitary specimen, a female, of this genus which I found on Depuy's spring creek at the end of August, 1994. Gustafson says the genus is quite common in Montana, but believes it is nocturnal, having captured many of them in his over-night light traps, near lakes.

Like the trico, the Caenis genus has a short life, hatching from egg to nymph in as little as five days, molting from dun to spinner in five to six minutes and living only a total of three or four hours.

A relatively new species of the genus (1984) is the C. youngi, which was discovered by Tom Young on Hebgen Lake. A paper on the new species was authored by George Roemhild, a biologist at Montana State University. Other of the same species have been found in lakes and ponds in south western Montana and also on Slough Creek in Yellowstone Park. My specimen has a pale cream or yellow abdomen which is quite thick and stubby compared to the the overall length of the fly which is 3/16". The thorax is a light tan with a touch of pink in it. Tails are gold.

I would suggest the following imitation:

Hook: Tiemco 100, 20.
Body: Eggshell Danville over white painted hook shank, built up slightly and

ribbed with fine, gold wire.
Thorax: Light brown with some pink in it.
Wing: White or dun with rusty edge,
divided, bunched and flattened.
Tail: Three barbs from golden pheasant
topping feather.

## Callibaetis nigritus

Just about every geometric shape you can think of...trapezoids, triangles, quadrangles, rectangles...even dots and dashes...are all part of the strange and unique design on the wings of the dun of the Callibaetis nigritus. And when the dun molts into the spinner seven to nine hours after emergence most of that design disappears as though scrubbed and washed off by the process. What we have left is what workers call vitta, a streak or band of color along the leading edge of the hyaline wing, which can be totally lacking on some males, but nearly always visible on females.

It's fairly easy to recognize a species of Callibaetis, but's it's not easy to say which one it is. The vitta can be heavy or thin. Spring adults can be twice as large as late summer ones. Bodies and legs will be sprinkled with small reddish or dark brown spots, but one species I observed had darker spots on the top of their abdomens than on the bottom. The speckled parts and vitta wings account for the angler's name; speckled dun or spinner.

It is difficult to give the preferred habitat of the genus. Some of my samples came from Hebgen lake, September 8, 1993, and from a private spring creek near Bozeman a few days after that. This is quite a slow moving, flat surfaced creek with some silt and sand-filled eddies. A few years ago, (long before I ever thought of this work), the same creek had a good hatch of Callibaetis and I had memorable fishing there with a new soft-hackled dun imitation. Dan Gustafson has collected C. nigritus from the Gallatin which can hardly be called a slow moving river, and that was in May, 1983. His samples are quite large measuring nearly 1/2 inch in the body and the same in the wing. There are two tails on the adult, although the nymph sports three, the center tail getting lost somehow in the emergence or molt.

In MAYFLIES OF MICHIGAN TROUT STREAMS, by Justin W. Leonard and Fannie A. Leonard, 1962, we find, "Nymphs of this genus are primarily lake-and-pond-dwellers, but sometimes occur in still-water areas in or adjacent to trout streams." And the following description of the nymphal habitat in MAYFLIES OF NORTH AND CENTRAL AMERICA, also places the home of the Callibaetis more in still water than running. "In still water such as permanent ponds, roadside ditches and margins of lakes or in transient pools. The nymphs show very wide limits of tolerance, occuring in great abundance in areas where the water is choked with vegetation, but also occurring in areas where vegetation is very sparse."

On July 3, 1994, my wife, Hazel, and I encountered a Callibaetis species on the tree-lined, tarred roads and parking lot of the Lewis Lake campground in Yellowstone Park. This was at least a quarter mile from the lake, but I had seen other spinners previously in their mating dances over tree-lined roads near other bodies of water. The roads must look like rivers or river channels to the spinners flying a few feet above them, or, perhaps they choose the more open areas because of higher visibility, although the areas over a lake or a river are just as open. This happened from 1 to 2 p.m. on a nice, sunny day. We walked down to the lake, which narrows into and becomes the Lewis River, where we could see quite a few fish feeding on Callibaetis spinners.

Even with its still-water stamp, Callibaetis is probably fished more in these parts on running water than on still, and during September 5, 6 and 7, 1994, the year of a major drought here in Montana, the genus seemed to be growing on moving water even more. One major river here was so low and choked with weeds and vegetation, that one or more species of Callibaetis was thriving on it as never before. "Low flow. High silt. Loss of habitat. Rapid growth of vegetation. That's not a good list. If a river system doesn't have a good spring flood or it's a flop, Callibaetis will have a head start in trying to find a good home for itself. They find new habitats in a short time, taking only 6 weeks or so to go from egg to spinner." says Gustafson.

He may be right. I have fished the river for several years during most months of the year and never noticed the insect there before. In '94, I saw mostly male spinners beginning at around 11 a.m. and lasting throughout most of the day. The spinners were everywhere on the river, near the banks and well out towards the middle of the river over the shallow riffles. Flight patterns seemed a little different from those near Lewis Lake. Here the spinners were lower, hovering then jerking forward repeatedly. The Lewis Lake spinners were quite high up, flew up on rapid wing beats and glided down on shimmering, still wings, which is more like the traditional pattern.

I had enough presence of mind to net a couple of the male spinners. The wings showed a little vitta on the leading edges, the rest of them being absolutely hyaline. The bodies were difficult to describe, particularly in the segments where there seemed to be a definite top and bottom. The top was a slate brown and the bottom a chalkish white, both sides sprinkled with reddish brown spots.

That evening I tied the following pattern on a size 16

Tiemco 100 dry fly hook. Body: Gray Danville with thin copper wire ribbing then coated with fly tying cement. Dark brown thorax. Rusty edge hackle. Three barbs of golden pheasant topping for the tail.

The next day was a copy of the previous one; hot and breezy. Callibaetis spinners came and here and there I found a trout feeding on them. Now, I will admit that perhaps any generic fly tied thin might have raised some of those trout. But the observation, readiness and a pattern based on the actual insect gave me confidence and joy. "Here, see this. You know it's a vitta-stripped Callibaetis. Looks good, doesn't it? Oh, you like it. Sorry, old boy." All fly fishing should be like that.

Tom Travis, owner of the Master Angler in Livingston, has fished Callibaetis with clients in the upper end of Depuy and he thinks they can be found on the deeper, slower parts of Armstrong and Nelson. He pointed out, however, that now, with many of the private lakes along the Yellowstone in Paradise Valley open to pay fishing, Callibaetis dun and spinner imitations will probably become more important to anglers visiting this area in the near future.

I also spoke to Bob Auger, river keeper at DePuy, in the late summer of 1994, and he said he saw more Callibaetis this year "due to the tremendous weed growth."

So, I have seen and, in some cases, photographed, Callibaetis spinners on five or six occasions over a period of three years, and fished a new pattern on the Montana river I spoke of earlier.

The formal dressing is as follows:

Hook:
Tiemco 100, 16.

Abdomen: Gray.

Thorax: Reddish brown.

Ribbing: Copper wire.

Hackle: White or off white, with one turn of partridge hackle in front.

You can also eliminate the partridge by dabbing the leading edge of the wing with a brown marker. (I have departed from the use of gold wire here because I thought the reddish copper wire might give the impression of the reddish spots on the abdomen.)

On September 3, 1995, just a short time before we started setting the type for the book, I fished a Callibaetis hatch on the Henry's Fork which should be described here. The activity started around 10 a.m., with the appearance of scattered Callibaetis on the surface and some large trout feeding on them. My partner thought the insects were duns because the wings were up and the dark, leading edges stood out like sticks. I caught a couple of the insects and found they were female spinners. But why were their wings up? Had they already mated? Had they already laid their eggs? Another day or two and I may have had the answers. Even so, I designed a pattern which I think would be an effective one whenever the same 'stick' winged Callibaetis appears in your neighborhood. Same body as above, thorax and spotted tail. Hackle/wing: darkish dun hackle with all the barbs pulled straight up above the hook, and left there. An alternate hackle/wing could be in the Glanrhos style where you take the hackle around the hook three or four times and leave the tip of the hackle standing straight up like a wing. For more information on the Glanrhos tie, see my SOFT-HACKLED FLY IMITATIONS.

## Centroptilum bifurcatum
*(Yellow Sulphur)*

In August and sometimes in the early part of September this small Baetidae will be an important food source for the trout of all three spring creeks near Livingston, Montana. I have also seen it on other spring creeks closer to Bozeman. Gustafson has specimens of it from the Gallatin, the Madison and other famous trout streams in the area. It is a small mayfly, in the size 20 range. The dun is a gorgeous creature in yellow and rosy orange, with small black eyes on the female which are plainly visible. The brilliant color of the species makes it look bigger than it really is. As a spinner, the fly is still stunning with hyaline wings and a body or abdomen which is also hyaline for the segments from 2 to 6 or 7. The last three segments will be reddish or brownish, especially on the male, which some workers say is the sperm showing through the abdomen wall. Gustafson agrees and he also thinks the color of female spinner abdomens is basically the color of the eggs inside her abdomen.

The clear or hyaline abdomen is a spinner trademark not only of the Centroptilum, but of the Baetis genus as well, which makes identifying without a microscope difficult. One major difference is found on the trailing edges of the forewing: In the Baetis there are two short, unattached veins called intercalaries between the major cross veins and in the Centroptilum there is only one. Some species of Stenonema, says Gustafson, also have hyaline abdomens.

Species of Centroptilum have not earned much space in the 'hatch' books, although there are more than 20 species described in MAYFLIES OF NORTH AND CENTRAL AMERICA. Only four of these are found in the northwest. Gustafson calls them "summer warm water critters which you'll find in the lower Gallatin." He also points out that some female duns of the Baetis species are bright yellowy orange.

Where the fisherman's name, yellow sulphur, for this fly comes from I cannot trace. The name is redundant and is not to be found in THE FISHERMAN'S HANDBOOK OF TROUT FLIES, although it lists two blue-winged sulphur flies. Marinaro wrote a chapter in A MODERN DRY-FLY CODE entitled "Blue-and Pale-Winged Sulphurs", in which he guessed they were of the Ephemerella genus. He admitted he could not name the insects to species because of a difficulty in collecting males. He complained, "Without a male spinner in good condition, a taxonomist cannot make a determination. The male spinners are rarely on the water and the few male duns that were collected failed to molt satisfactorily in the cages." Nothing much has changed in that department among mayfly workers. Marinaro suggested tying the fly in two sizes, 16 and 20, so he was in the ball park on the size of one of the flies.

C. bifurcatum emerges on the spring creeks in the early afternoon on some days and throughout the afternoon and into the evening on other days. It has a relatively short molting time of ten to twelve hours, so it's quite possible that the fly can present itself to trout as a dun and as a spinner in the same fishing day.

The short molting time also suggests that spinners will be mixed with duns. On Depuy, the spinner is suggested in the early a.m., and evening.

I collected species of this fly by sweeping the weeds with a net along the banks of Armstrong and DePuy spring creeks during August, 1994. I also saw duns on the water. At times, the emergence coincides with that of the PMD, and even though it is two sizes bigger, it could be mistaken for the sulphur because of its yellowy green color. Below the blue gate on DePuy, I watched one PMD scud across the surface to my bank where he got out of the water by climbing up some vegetation saving himself the trouble of flying away to it, which is the normal method.

Whenever possible throughout this book, I have attempted to fish the new, suggested spinner or dun/spinner for obvious reasons. I had permission to study and collect on all three spring creeks for which I was very grateful. When I saw the Centroptilums on Armstrong and after I designed the first version, I asked Allyn O'Hair, the owner, if I could try it out during the next few evenings, particularly since most anglers left the creek long before dark.

He gave me permission and on July 29 I started fishing at 7:30 with the first of the new Centroptilum imitations. No other angler was on the river. It was a quiet, lovely time of the day with little wind and overcast sky. I started just above the changing lean to and picnic table in the rather wide and deep flat which always seems to have several trout showing. I would hate to guess how many artificial flies have been coaxed down through this water, the blueprint of them and the real thing firmly implanted in the heads of every trout in it. They look so easy, perhaps even friendly because they let you get so close. One thinks a short reach cast, 7x leader, no drag on the fly. Bingo! That's what you think! Instead it's refusal after refusal, the trout with head up just under that obvious fake, often following it a foot or more to check the fisherman's knot...improved clinch or Turle....before returning to his spot and devouring the next natural with gusto.

Well, I never had any of that! There was something in the fly...in the body...in the hackle...in the tail. To seven trout that evening, that artificial was the real thing. And I started to glow thinking I had stumbled on to this irresistable yellow sulfur. Before I catch another trout, I thought, I'd better retire it to immortality, when number eight broke me and took the fly. In the fading light, I replaced it with another and caught another two, a total of ten hooked and nine landed in one hour and forty five minutes.

During the two years, up to that time, I worked on this book, I dreamed of a fly like this, a dressing I could hand my readers which, itself, could easily be worth the price of the book. Then, my conscience started acting up and the longer I thought about it, the more I began to think it might be unfair to the trout. So, I am not giving that dressing.

I am giving, instead, the following dressing for the yellow sulphur:

Hook: Tiemco 100 , 20 , painted white for maximum brightness and see-through quality.
Abdomen: Yellow Danville.
Thorax: Pink fur.
Hackle: White or dun with rusty edge or brightest ginger you can find.
Tail: Golden pheasant.

Those of you astute in trout fly history will recognize the famous Tups Indispensible in this pattern. So be it; it's time someone brought it back in honor of G.E.M. Skues.

## Drunella coloradensis, *(Western green drake)*
## Siphlonurus occidentalis, *(Gray drake)*

Perhaps no other writing in this book sums up the reason for it better than this chapter on the spinners of the so-called western green drake and gray drake. The two species are included in the same chapter because they were found simultaneously on the same part of the Yellowstone river in the national park. They are approximately the same size and have nearly the same coloring. Both wing pairs are hyaline. And it's quite possible one or the other artificials could be fished successfully for both species, even though the gray drake is a light, reddish brown and the western green drake is yellowy green.

The time of this report is from around August 1, 1994, when a guide told me his clients fished the gray drake on the river, to August 16, when a friend and I fished new spinners imitating both species; and to a day in July, 1995, when I fished the gray drake spinner on the Henry's Fork. Hazel, my wife and I did the leg work on August 12, 13 and 14, 1994, observing and photographing both species and fishing some new experimental patterns with only moderate success. Dan Gustafson identified the spinners, all females, on August 15, 1994, and it was then that I designed the spinner imitations you'll find in this chapter.

What I hope to show here is that there aren't enough spinner patterns in American fly fishing and that a great deal of high quality sport is lost because of it. I believe we have too many generic flies and not enough specific species flies. This comes from the desire to find one fly which will work anywhere and anytime. We all know that's impossible.

The gray drake and western green drake are popular with anglers in many parts of the United States and are not confined just to Yellowstone National Park. Yet, it is difficult to find gray drake and western green drake spinner patterns and many other specific species spinner patterns in the catalogs of some of the most prestigious fly shops in the country. One of the largest western companies shows five spinners. No drakes. A popular Pennsylvania shop shows four. No drakes. A Seattle-based shop lists five. No drakes. That's the way it goes from one catalog to another. I hate to say this, but most catalogs show more grasshopper patterns than they do spinners. There's not one shop in Bozeman that has these spinners available and they are difficult, if not impossible to find even in West Yellowstone. It could be true that certain anglers are using specific gray drake and western green drake spinners, but they're tying the patterns themselves from their own study and observation.

Currently, and from my observation, the rusty spinner is the most popular in American fly fishing. It is merely a continuation of the earlier English favorite, the red spinner or red quill, which was included in the chapter on the history of spinners. Then and now, the rusty spinner is a good pattern because the body color is representative of the reddish brown assumed by many mayflies in the spinner stage. The rusty spinner could work as a gray drake and western green drake spinner, but you'd have to tie it yourself on a big enough hook, because it is rarely available in anything larger than a 16.

But let's look at the spinners themselves. We'll start with the gray drake, S. occidentalis, which may, in the dun stage, appear gray to anglers, but has very little gray in the spinner stage. It's a brown, medium-sized mayfly, strikingly marked with obvious ringlike segments. Body length is from 7/16" to 9/16". Wings are hyaline, slightly longer than the body. There are two, light spotted tails, 1 and 1/2 the length of the body. The bottom side of the abdomen is pale lavender with a purple horseshoe design on every segment. The top side of the abdomen is a shade of translucent brown through which the horseshoes can barely be seen.

The Drunella coloradensis, formerly Ephemerella, or western green drake is a trifle shorter, from 7/16" to 1/2", but with a stockier appearance than the gray drake. Wings are hyaline. Body is lighter colored, leaning more towards yellow or yellowish brown. Abdomen segments are dramatically ringed in a chalkish white which accentuates the striped pattern. Stripes. Stripes. Stripes. That's what you think of when you see these spinners and that's why they are an important body, design element in the spinner patterns in this book.

The gray drake dressing:

Hook: Tiemco 109 BL, 13.
Body: Flymaster light brown thread, (coffee),
ribbed with medium gold wire,
coated with fly tying cement.
Thorax: Medium brown, at least one third
larger in diameter than abdomen.
Wing: Three or four strands of organza
with light dun or rusty edged or ginger
hackle behind.
Tail: 3 or 4 barbs of golden pheasant
topping feather.

The western green drake dressing:

Hook: Tiemco 109 BL, 13.
Body: Flymaster light olive, ribbed with medium gold wire, coated with fly tying cement.
Thorax: Dark olive, at least one third larger in diameter than abdomen.
Wing: Two or three strands organza with white or dun with rusty edge hackle behind the organza. A light dun or ginger hackle can also be used.
Tail: 3 or 4 barbs of golden pheasant topping feather.

To flatten the hackle as a spinner wing, turn the vice towards you and separate and stroke the barbs on both sides of the hook with wetted or waxed thumbs and forefingers.

It's not often that the studies of spinners in this book turn out as well rounded and complete as in this chapter on the two drakes. I found the spinners. They were identified. I designed the imitations, and fished them with great success. The following is the report on some of the fishing.

I asked a friend, Jesse Lair, if he would like to try them out with me at the same place my wife and I found them on the Yellowstone. There was no way of knowing, two days later, August 16, 1994, if the spinners would still be on the water, but at around six p.m., the first gray and western green drake spinners appeared and the cutts took active notice of them.

The Yellowstone this year, 1994, was at the lowest of many years and we were able to fish the best part of a long, rapid bend which would not be fly fishable at normal water levels. Jesse, armed with the gray drake spinner, had first crack at a fish which required a very long cast. His first attempt was short. He moved closer and lengthened the cast and was still short. One more step closer and a little more line and Jesse had the first trout ever caught on this spinner pattern.

I had stopped fishing to watch his performance, but now I, too, fishing the new, western green drake spinner, had a choice of two or three rising Yellowstone river cutthroat and I picked the closest, which was almost straight across from me, requiring little line manipulation for a drag-free float over him. There was no hesitation. No doubt. He took it and with so little stuff on the hook, it went in.

The nice thing about fishing a big river like the Yellowstone is that you can try two, three or even four fish without moving too much. They can be in front of you, on both sides of you and even behind you. And I caught another two fish on the new spinner before moving down stream to wider, but slower water.

On the way, I was looking downstream into the sun and saw a cutt rise right in the reflection of it. I pulled some line off the reel, cast short and started paying out line, hoping I was keeping up sufficiently to prevent drag. I was. The trout practically impinged himself and he was number four.

I took four more. I never changed the fly and I never dressed it. A couple false casts between business casts were enough to dry the fly sufficiently to keep it quite visible even at 30 and 40 feet away. When the fly was in the fish's lane he took it for the real thing. It was one of the most satisfying fishing experiences I ever had, and I found out later it was the same for Jesse.

"Why didn't you continue to fish after you caught

the first cutt on the new fly?"

"I didn't want to spoil anything. It was perfect the way it was."

I had another opportunity to test the gray drake spinner the following year, in July, 1995, on a portion of the Henry's Fork. Mike Langford, who guides for Mike Lawson in Last Chance, ID, called to tell me the river was thick with S. occidentalis spinners. Mike had worked nearly 28 straight days and was anxious to hook some trout himself. I took the oars of the guide boat myself and let Mike be the first to try the gray drake spinner. The standard guide boat dry fly pattern on this water at this time is a thickly tied, size 12 Adams. Don't ask me why the fly works. The color is wrong. The thinking could have been as simple as, "hey, gray drake, the gray-colored Adams." The design is wrong, like a worm or egg sack is wrong. There is a lot of so-called dry fly fishing in this country with generics just like this. "I use nothing but the dry fly," the angler says puffing up his chest. But he has no more idea why the fly is taken than the man in the moon. Go back to Halford, "To define dry-fly fishing, I should describe it as presenting to the rising fish the best possible imitation of the insect on which he is feeding in its natural position." By no stretch of the wildest imagination could anyone claim that the Adams is the "best possible imitation" of the gray drake spinner. You could argue the Adams is the best imitation for the gray drake because more people use it and it works. But, quite possibly, until this day, and on that water, nobody ever tried an artifical spinner tied to look more closely like the imago of the S. occidentalis.

Some fish were working near enough to the bank to be fished from so I rowed over to it. Mike spotted a fish and went up the bank after it. It was a big fish, and like many of that size, moved around quite a bit, taking the spent flies at four or five different locations. At times, he went further out in the stream than Mike could reach, but would always return to a spot close enough. I don't think the average angler could have got the fly to this fish, without drag, but Mike did and the fish took the S. occidentalis imitation with no show of doubt or hesitancy. I also think Mike was skeptical, but now into this big fish, he was smiling broadly, enjoying the long runs and hearing the screeching of the reel. It was not an easy fight but very few fish win with Mike and after several minutes worked it down to the guide boat where I netted it with the long-handled boat net. Mike measured it, a rainbow, using the oblong side of the hoop of the net which measures 23 inches. And the trout took up every inch.

We counted 6 other fish hooked with the new spinner, including one which I hooked, but did not land. And I had a rare spinner experience on the river which made the trip with Mike even more worth while.

Further downstream in faster water, I began to see the mating dances of the S. occidentalis male spinners. They hovered in the warm air from four to ten feet, without much up and down movement of other species. The two tails were wide spread, almost perpendicular to the long, slender bodies. The insects were quite close to the bank, which shortens the distance the copulating couples must travel in order to get 'unhooked' after copulation. This is necessary because the female must get back to the water to lay her fertilized eggs and the male may want to join the dancing males to try the whole thing over again.

Anchored here in Mike's new Hyde guide boat, I saw two pairs of copulating couples land, one in an inch of rainwater in the center of the boat, and the other on the light gray fore-deck. The first couple separated quickly, the male drowning in the rainwater, the female flying off. The second couple landed on their sides, still connected, on the smooth fiber glass where I could see them as plain as day. In may fly literature, I had seen drawings of copulating couples and the view of the two insects was just like the drawings. The male's, long front legs were bent up and backward over the female's thorax, and his abdomen was severly bent upwards joining the underside of the female's 8th or 9th abdomen segment. His two tails were divided around her abdomen, which, now, makes me wonder what the three-tailed species does with the odd tail.

I watched the couple separate, which did not appear easy, and now I could plainly see little differences in each sex. The male appeared harder, was a little smaller, and more streamlined and now I could see his claspers. The female appeared softer and was larger in width and length, with more red in her body than the male.

In a short time, they flew away and I think the pair left more of an impression on me than Mike's 23 inch rainbow.

# Drunella flavilinea

*(Formerly Ephemellera flavilinea)*

It is usually true that when a mayfly receives an anglers' nickname, it has done so because of its popularity. And 'flav', short for D. flavilinea, is a word that pops up frequently among anglers in California, Idaho, Montana, Oregon, Washington, Wyoming and Yellowstone National Park. In various workers' biologies, the flav is also found in British Columbia, and is allied to D. coloradensis, although the coloradensis, or western green drake, is at least one hook size bigger than the flav, and the flav will have very pale wing venation, where it is much more noticeable in the bigger fly.

Both species share the same rivers which are medium to large size and which have rapid flow, over rocks, gravel and debris, although the flav seems to prefer the lower parts where water temperatures are higher.

For this chapter, I had to borrow a flav, a male, in alcohol from Dan Gustafson which was captured from the Gallatin on the 29th of June, 1988. I made several attempts to get my own insects, duns or spinners, during the summer of 1994, but failed. Once on the Firehole, I had 15 or so flav duns in a screened shoe box sitting in a shaded section of my partner's car. He did not know I had placed them there and moved the car, and went back out into the river to continue fishing. The new position brought the sun's rays directly onto the box and the duns perished.

On July 18, 1994, I heard there were flavs on the Madison river near the "Three dollar bridge," and that they were coming off as duns in the late afternoon. At around 6:45 p.m. I saw the first of them coming down among the boulders close to the bank where most of the fishing on this part of the Madison takes place. Fish became quite active and I saw a couple take a few duns. I netted 8 or 10 and brought them home for molting, but nothing ever happened. I did measure the duns, however. The bright olive green body was 5/16" long and the dark, smoky dun wings were a little longer. On the water, the duns looked top heavy with wings too large for their bodies. I think a dun/spinner, as described in other chapters of this book, might be in order:

Hook: Tiemco 100,14.
Body: Danville light olive,
ribbed with gold wire.
Thorax: Dark green or olive, not too thick.
Hackle: Dark dun, tied thickly.
Tail: Four or five strands of clear lureflash
about the same length as the body.

The flav spinner is quite a delicate critter with wings which have no substance to them at all. The wings of most spinners, even though they are hyaline, do give off some color because of the venation. On the flav, it is very pale. There are not many cross veins and the few longitudinal ones are set wide apart. Because of this, I'm suggesting a pattern which has no hackle for wings, only a few strands of organza which should give the impression of a clear wing and which might help hold the fly near the surface for a short time. Here is the tie:

Hook: Tiemco 100, 16.
Body: Coffee with thin gold rib.
Thorax: Dark brown with a little red in it.
Hackle: 5 or 6 single strands of organza,
tied in front of the thorax then
trimmed slightly longer than the body.
Tail: 3 barbs golden pheasant topping twice
the length of the body.

This pattern approaches the transparent jenny spinner of J. C. Mottram, who said, "...one of the best ways of indicating transparency is to omit the transparent parts altogether"; and the no-wing spinner of Swisher/Richards, which is tied without any wings at all. It would be worth experimenting with a spinner like this in other patterns, particularly in the smaller sizes and with the lightest hook one could find.

# Drunella grandis, *Formerly Ephemerella*
## *(Green Drake)*

As families and genera of mayflies grow over the years, in professional, taxonomic literature, they become unwieldy and unmanageable. From time to time, a family or genus will be revised by workers who take species from one genus and move them into another. The genus Ephemerella for example, of which the green drake in this chapter was a species for many years, had more than 100 species in it at the time of the revision in 1962. So, fifteen of these species, including the grandis or green drake, were placed in the uncrowded subgenus Drunella.

Green Drake, as we all know, is a popular angler's name for more than one species of large, green mayfly. In England, the name is used for the Ephemera danica. In the eastern US, it is used for the Ephemera guttulata. And here, of course, it is used for the Drunella grandis, formerly Ephemerella grandis.

In either species it is a big, exciting fly for the trout and for the trout fisherman. The reason, of course, is that it brings big fish to the feed. And where you've not fished anything bigger than a 14 or maybe a 12 so far into the year, you can throw out a green drake on a 10 or 8 and see it taken even if you have less than perfect vision. To me, the fish seems to show more of himself, taking green drakes than he does taking size 16 PMDs.

At least, so it seemed on the Henry's Fork, on opening day this year, June 15, 1994. Standing on the east bank, I could see trout feeding on green drake duns clear across the river, a hundred yards wide. The job was to get to within casting distance before someone else beat you to it. The only fish I was able to reach, I took on the first cast with one of my new, green drake dun/spinners. The same fly also produced fish for Catherine and Laurent Dobler, who were visiting me from France and who wanted to take part in the new fly experiment on the Henry's Fork.

The dun/spinner patterns in this book, as the name implies are suggested to be used as duns and as spinners,with far more opportunity to fish the green drake as a dun than a spinner. In fact, few people have ever seen D. grandis spinners on or near the Henry's Fork in natural surroundings. How and when and where the duns molt remain a mystery even to the professional workers. No one has ever recorded a male mating dance, or documented a female laying eggs. I asked experienced Henry's Fork river guides, Steve Mates, Mike Langford and others if they ever witnessed green drake spinners and they all said they saw only few specimens in the many years they worked on the river. I, myself, photographed a female green drake spinner with a ball of blue green eggs on the antenna of my car 8 or 10 years ago. The car was parked next to the Henry's Fork above the Ranch at Last Chance.

So, how does the green drake propogate itself? Gustafson suggests the following. They mate at night. They mate at high altitudes. They mate at great distances from the river. Gustafson also points out that green drakes have short, synchronous emergence periods, which they have developed through evolution as a means of overwhelming their predators. A big insect like the green drake not only attracts fish and fishermen, but every manner of bird capable of hovering over the river. On Henry's Fork this year, I saw grackles feed on the duns all day long. They worked from a series of three rocks set in a loose triangle. Their vision was astounding, flying 75 feet or more between the rocks to pick up this or that dun. I believed they could easily have eaten their weight in duns before the day was over.

Synchronous emergence can be seen as a sharp pointed rise in a curve in which a number of duns get nailed at the beginning and end of the rise. At the height of the rise there is such an onslaught of duns that it's impossible for the predators to get all of them. "Big animals like green drakes are highly prized by predators and the short emergence period helps improve the odds of survival for the insect," says Gustafson, "the secret of where and when the spinners mate and when they lay the fertilized eggs on the Henry's Fork may also be part of their protection program."

It's interesting that there are other, similar mysteries in the world of mayfly entomology. In an article in the May 1993 FLY FISHERMAN, Dick Pobst writes about a 'gray drake' hatch of which only the spinner can be found. "...we have seen millions of these spinners, but now comes the real enigma: We have seen practically no duns, emergers or nymphs. Oh, we can find a few, but precious few," says Pobst. Rumors in Michigan have it that Pobst is offering a handsome reward to anyone who can solve the puzzle or come up with twenty or thirty nymphs and duns.

The green drake hatch on the Henry's Fork lasted about three days this year (1994). (Smaller mayflies like Baetis tricaudatus may hatch over a period of months.) I was able to capture many duns, only four of which, two males and two females molted successfully. This took about 48 hours.

The spinners are strikingly beautiful, with clear

wings and thick abdomens and heavy, dark thoraxes. The most distinguishing feature is the pronounced striping between the segments of the abdomen, bringing a zebra to mind. In BIOLOGY OF MAYFLIES, 1935, the same feature is described, "Abdominal segments dark purplish brown with wide pale margins, so as to appear conspicuously ringed." In the 1962 revision of the genus by Allen and Edmunds, "Terga largely purplish brown with pale pleural and posterior margins, giving a distinct ringed appearance to the abdomen."

There is little green in the whole insect, although the base of the wings has a yellowy green cast to it, which is very prominent on the dun. The spinner appears green perhaps because of the pale yellow stripes between the dark, purply brown segments. Body length is 3/4". Three tails almost twice as long. Wings: hyaline, with a span of 1 and 1/2".

Until recently there have not been many hooks which were properly designed for big spinners like the green drake. The length in the the shank was lacking. In standard configurations, the hooks were too heavy. Most long shank hooks were designed for streamers and were also too heavy to remain in the film surface. Now, Tiemco has come out with a hook which seems just right for big duns and spinners. It is the barbless, black BL 109, which offers a wide gape, extra fine wire and a variable long shank, (large sizes, 7 and 9 are 3x long; sizes 11 through 19 are 1x long.) The size 11 with a shank length of ll/16" seems ideal for the green drake spinner and dun/spinner in this book.

In designing these flies, I have concentrated on the most visual distinction of the imago which is the abdominal stripping. The green drake also has a heavy, thick body which requires other than just tying thread to build up the imitation. So, the body is built up slightly by the tying thread, 6x or 3x, followed by a single layer of Orvis dark green flexi-floss, or Lagartun floss, which is then ribbed with doubled, gold wire or thin, flat gold, and coated with fly tying cement. A heavy, dark brown thorax is added.

To tie the dun/spinner, add a darkish blue dun hackle and to tie the spinner add a white or off white cock or hen hackle. To finish the spinner, and with the fly still in the vice, turn the hook towards you and grab equal portions of the hackles in your thumbs and forefingers and separate them into a flat plane.

This is not the first mention in fly fishing literature of a pattern which might be used as a dun and as a spinner. There is the Jorgen-Betts Extended body, green drake spinner/dun, which, because of its name, must be meant to fish either way.

Extended body flies have been with us for many years. There were several patterns in Halford's FLOATING FLIES AND HOW TO DRESS THEM, 1886, including some very large flies for the green, brown and gray drakes. The major advantage of the extended body is the use of a smaller, lighter hook on which to dress the fly. The major disadvantage is constructing the body from some material which is soft enough to feel like a mayfly's body in the mouth of a trout, yet, which can be constructed and worked on during its manufacture.

John Foust, who had a fly shop and guide service in Hamilton, MT., ties beautiful and effective extended body green drakes and brown drakes, using dyed deer or elk hair for the extended body. His flies are tied parachute style with a white poly flag in the center of the chute which is held up during the hackling by a tool he designed for the job. His size 12 Green Drake has a body which is 3/4" long, while the actual shank length of the hook is only 3/8" long. He claims and is probably right this kind of fly is more bouyant with less weight.

I was fortunate enough to float about nine miles of the Bitteroot with Foust on June 28, 1994. Green Drakes were still supposed to be on the river and we did see a handful at the beginning of the trip. I fished his extended body green drake for more than half the trip, then switched to one of my new, green drake spinner patterns which took a big fish. We had a pleasant day's fishing proving that green drakes were still fresh in the minds of the rainbows of the beautiful Bitteroot river.

# Epeorus albertae

Only four species of this genus of the Heptageniidae family are known to exist in Montana, and I found only a single female adult of one of them on a private spring creek near my home in August, 1993. Gustafson, for his doctor's thesis, ECOLOGY OF AQUATIC INSECTS IN THE GALLATIN RIVER DRAINAGE, 1990, collected all four; albertae, deceptivus, grandis and longimanus, from various parts of that river. The thesis shows the preference of the species for the different habitats offered by the river. Gustafson called them 'longitudinal zones', ranging them from the larger, warmer, main-stem of the river, downstream of Bozeman to the smallest, coldest high mountain creeks in Yellowstone Park. In the thesis are also 'abundance codes' which give relative numbers of each species found in the various 'zones', and ranging from 'absent' to 'abundant'. For example, E. albertae was reported to be abundant only in the lower sections of the river; E. deceptivus was found in moderate numbers in only the higher portions of the river; E. grandis, the biggest species of the genus, was found in all but the bottom two zones; and E. longimanus was found in relatively strong numbers in all but lowest and highest zones.

Gustafson found 7 families, 23 genera and 58 species of the mayfly in the Gallatin river. The thesis also includes the study of the plecoptera, trichoptera, diptera and coleoptera, the collection of which he compares to the ephemeroptera. "Contrary to the situation with both the Plecoptera and the Trichoptera, Ephemeroptera species are better inventoried by collecting the nymphs than by collecting the adults. The adults can usually be reared when necessary for identification. Only 61% of the species known from the drainage were taken as swarming adults and several of these were only very rarely encountered. The mayflies of lower elevation streams are more frequently encountered as swarming adults than are those of cold, mountain streams."

Comparing my two years of collecting on many streams to his several years of collecting on just the one, I estimate my percentage of species taken as swarming adults to be far less than 50%. I did not have nymph rearing facilities, so I captured duns instead and watched them molt into spinners. It's interesting that duns have virtually no interest to workers like Gustafson (except when he is fishing); they identify only through the nymph and the male adult.

Since my female spinner came from a spring creek downstream of Bozeman, it could be placed in either the albertae or longimanus species groups. The body is 5/16" long with an almost clear abdomen and tannish thorax. Wings are hyaline. There are two spotted tails, twice the length of the body.

The imitations could be tied as follows:
Hook: Tiemco 100, 16.
Body: Eggshell Danville over white painted hook shank, ribbed with fine gold wire and coated with fly tying cement. Light tan dubbed thorax.
Wing: Honey dun or light ginger hackle.
Tail: Three barbs golden rooster topping feather, twice the length of the body.

Some writers have associated species of Epeorus to the ancient pink lady trout fly, which used to be tied with a pink floss body. Danville makes a fluorescent pink thread, but I have not had good results with fluorescent thread bodies. Other pink thread could be substituted for the eggshell, or a light pink dubbing could be used instead of the light tan.

# Ephemera simulans
*(Brown Drake)*

Even though the brown drake is as big as the green drake, it does not seem to suffer from the short emergence character of the green drake. I found the brown drake on the Henry's Fork as early as June 6, 1994 and as late as June 17, 1994, and heard about its appearance on that river even after that. True, one doesn't see the brown drake on the water in nearly the same numbers as the green, but it's fishable longer which might make it more important to the angler.

There is also no mystery connected to the brown drake life cycle. Nymphs, duns and male and female spinners are observable and catchable and male mating dances are quite common. My wife and I saw a huge male spinner display on the Henry's Fork on June 6 which is worth talking about. We heard about it through Brian Ramsey who worked for Mike Lawson in Last Chance, Idaho. We agreed to meet in the parking lot at 6 p.m.

This was at least 200 yards from the river, but when we got there, the males were dancing right over the tops of the cars. As high as 20 feet and as low as 10 feet. Beating, blurring wings to go up and the free ride down on stationary wings. Up and down innumerable times. I have never come across an adequate etymological explanation of the word 'spinner', but now I'm sure it must have evolved from many persons seeing the males dancing and appearing to be spinning in mid air. They truly are not spinning, but flying in place or hovering. However, the word, 'spinner' is better than the word, 'hover', or we'd have artificials like the 'rusty hover' and instead of a 'spinner fall', a 'hover fall'. In either case, all that can be seen are the bodies, which on the brown drake, are long and slender, equally as long as the green drake, but not so thick and not so conspicuously striped.

Brian and I had agreed he would fish an experimental brown drake spinner (I didn't have an Idaho license yet) and I handed him the solitary speciman. It was tied on a size 12 up eye mayfly hook made in England and sold by Veniard. The hook shank length is 1/2" and the wire could be called 'dry fly'. The fly was made with a clear lureflash tail, thin, gold wire ribbing and a slim body of brown Pearsall thread, coated with fly tying cement. The thorax was dark brown with a tinge of red in it. For the hackle, I used a Hoffman light gray, rooster hackle, divided after being wound on and pulled and formed into two halves on each side of the hook.

We had to leave Brian to his 'work' but he called the next day and told me what happened. "The fly worked really well. People beside me wondered what I was using. I hooked 8 good fish, with one in the 18 to 20 inch class. Other anglers were getting weird refusals and were not having as much luck."

Brian also thought the experimental fly was being taken for a dun, although both duns and spinners were on the water simultaneously. I saw them and netted them before I left. There were many male spinners on the water, too, not always with wings spent, but often with one wing flat on the water, and the other upright. That's a good time for a spinner tied in the Glanrhos style which I wrote about in my last book and which I have also included instructions for in this book. There are other mayfly species which have simultaneous or nearly simultaneous dun hatches and spinner falls. I've recorded such a situation in the chapter on Drunella flavilinea. I'm sure there are more than we know about and I'm sure that in many dun hatches there might be a few spinners of the same or other species mixed in. There has to be some overlapping and the longer the hatch of duns lasts, the greater the chance there will be some spinners in it.

But, weather and low temperatures do slow down the molting process or can prohibit the dun from ever turning into a spinner. On February 28, 1994, I captured two sets of baetis duns from Armstrong spring creek. One set was brought home to my office and the other was left in a live box placed in some weeds near the creek bank. In my office the baetis turned in to spinners in about 26 hours, while the ones left near the creek never molted. The first night's outdoor temperature went down to 30 and apparently it was low enough to prevent the duns from molting.

On the day after, I did the same thing and waited 30 hours for the 'outdoor' duns to molt, gave up and brought them home where they, too, molted in the relatively balmy 70 degree office.

The dressing for the brown drake spinner is pretty much the same as the green drake. Hook: Tiemco BL 109 size 11. Tail: 3 barbs of wood duck flank feather. Body: built up first into a taper by dark brown tying silk, then covered with a single layer of Orvis brown Flexi-Floss, or Lagartun French floss, ribbed by thin gold wire, coated with fly tying cement. Thorax: Dark brown with a touch of red in it. (The body and thorax should be kept thin and streamlined.) Hackle: White or off white, or light ginger, separated into two halves on each side of the hook then dabbed with a brown marker pen on the left and right wings to simulate the "numerous dark blotches and many margined cross veins," found on the simulans.

Armed with several of these new brown drake flies, Catherine and Laurent Dobler from France and I fished the middle section of the Henry's Fork on June 17, 1994. We were not there alone, because the word had got out that it was fishing better than the top part. We got to the water by around 10:30 and waited for something to happen. Some anglers were already in the center of the river, where they had waded to from the other side.

We were expecting to see green drakes and we thought we saw the first ones around 11. I waded out with my aquarium net and got the first one. It was a brown drake and for the rest of the day, all the big flies on that water were the same and the big trout were on them.

We waded out to the center of the river and joined at least 6 other anglers in a sort of large, scattered, semi-circle already in position. I must say that for four or five hours of fishing together, no one ever trespassed against another and very often we could hear someone ask, "Are you fishing that guy on your left?" before throwing his imitation to it.

Everyone, it appeared, had fish on. Big fish. Catherine had one on the new spinner. Laurent was a little slow getting started but caught onto the effectiveness of the American style, downstream, reach cast and hooked and landed four or five. I had around the same number, but I can remember only one, who broke me on the take, and who, after two or three minutes, jumped a prodigious height right in the middle of the semi-circle for everyone to see and laugh at, waited another three or four minutes and jumped again, repeating the jumps and the intervals 8 times before quitting and sulking off to some remote, more quiet corner of the Henry's Fork.

# Ephemerella inermis

*(Pale Morning Dun)*

I probably captured more PMD's than any other may-fly during my first year of collecting in 1993. They are every where in the west and northwest, including the state of Washington and even Alaska, and they have been collected by workers as far south as Arizona. The fly appears from the first of June through the end of September. Pale Morning Dun was the name given to at least two Ephemerella species, inermis and infrequens, by Swisher and Richards.

Ephemerella inermis was first reported in 1884 by the Reverend Eaton from a male and female adult collected in central Colorado and sent to him in England. Allen and Edmunds, also two well-known workers, say, "The adults swarm in very late evening and the females have been observed ovipositing during mid-morning, about 9:00 to 11:00 a.m. Numerous broods seem to occur throughout the summer months, but the population in the Green River (Utah) consists of a single brood that emerges in June and early July."

My greatest and most concentrated experience with PMD spinners occurred from the middle of July to the middle of August, 1993, on a private spring creek not too far from my home in Bozeman. At first, I started visiting the creek by one or two o'clock in the afternoon when I saw and netted many duns. In captivity, they usually molted in 24 hours or a little longer which meant, perhaps in natural conditions, spinners (from the previous day's production of duns) could be expected an hour or two after the emergence of the duns. And it was generally true. I would see duns first, then spinners with "U" shaped curves near the tail and then spinners with blue green egg sacks on the inside of the curves, after which the spinners would dive into the riffle to plant their eggs. I saw few mating pairs, so where they actually mated, I cannot say. As the summer progressed and got warmer, I visited the spring creek later and later and found the PMD duns still hatching at five and six o'clock with spinners still coming at seven and eight.

Which brings us to one of the major difficulties in trying to set dates and times for finding and fishing spinners, and perhaps, the major reason why no one has ever attempted a book on the subject before. There can never be the same number of spinners (except, perhaps for the trico) for trout to feed upon as the same number of duns of a given day's hatch. The reason is the tremendous loss of of duns to trout, to birds, to weather and to the vicissitudes of the molting process, itself. And the longer the molt takes, the greater must be the loss of spinner life in the waiting.

For example, I wondered how many duns might get eaten by trout in one, fairly confined pool of DePuy's spring creek, where one person could count the number of duns entering the pool and another could count the number of duns leaving it. I had the kind permission of the DePuys to study and collect mayflies on the creek, (on Armstrong and Nelson, as well) and I chose April 28, 1993, a nice, warmish day, from 12:30 to 1:30, to make the count.

My wife, Hazel, counted at the head and I counted at the tail. There were at least 6 good-sized trout visibly feeding on the Baetis duns in the pool. My wife counted 396 duns entering and I counted 60 leaving, a loss of some 336 duns in that one pool, during just one hour of the hatch!

Now, this is not a scientific way to conduct numerical experiments. There are too many variables. You could count insects twice, specially those coming in. What about the duns hatching in the pool itself? Some duns would surely fly off after entering the pool. We all have watched trout stuff themselves on duns and we've seen birds with beaks jammed with mayflies, still trying for more. We know without counting there is going to be a big difference in the number of insects which hatch and the number of the same clan which will live long enough to continue the species.

Dun emergence timing is always more predictable than the timing of spinner mating or egg laying because nymphs in water are not affected as much by air temperature or weather conditions which could delay or speed up the final molt of the dun to spinner. The dun comes, with weather ready or not and frequently we're fishing hatches in rain and snow and high winds, while it's rare to fish spinners in any but dry and warm and usually pleasant weather.

So, there is some indication with the PMD that we should fish spinner patterns of the insect during the hatch of duns as well as during spinner mating and egg laying. That is all the time. This is a good idea because even the dun of the PMD is a light, airy, creamy yellow, see-through kind of mayfly. Dominant body color of the spinner is best matched with Flymaster light olive on a white painted size 16 and 18 hook. Painting the hook white, of course, was the idea of John Dunne, and I'm suggesting the same process for the lighter colored bodies of the spinners in this book. With the darker bodied flies, I don't think painting the hook shank is necessary to hide it. Dunne's method was to dip the hook in the paint, eye first, then stick the eye into a bar of soap to dry. This meant cleaning the eye before tying.

My method is to stick the hook into a wine bottle cork

by the point and paint the shank only with a bodkin or needle point.

Here is the formal dressing:

Hook: Tiemco 100, 16, painted white.
Abdomen: Light olive, ribbed with fine gold wire, coated with fly tying cement or fast drying nail polish.
Thorax: Pale yellow.
Hackle: Rusty or reddish ginger.
Tail: 2 or 3 barbs golden pheasant topping feather.

Many anglers and fly tyers have erroneously claimed the PMD spinner to be the rusty spinner. The spinner body is only slightly darker than that of the dun, hence the choice of light olive.

# Epheron album

*(The White Fly)*

E. leukon, closely related and only other member of the Epheron genus, appears to have been the first American mayfly made known to science. This was in 1802, in Philadelphia, at a meeting of the American Philosophical Society. The paper, read by Dr. Hugh Williamson, included a recognizable description of the species and the following observations. "They begin to rise out of the (Passaic) river 35 or 40 minutes after the sun sets and continue rising about 15 minutes...The chrysalis deposits a thin white pellicle or skin on the surface of the water and rises a perfect insect. It continues on the wing an hour and perishes...The female drops two clusters of eggs upon the water and perishes immediately. The eggs are yellow. Each cluster is nearly one quarter of an inch in length and the thickness of a common pin, resembling the roe of a fish and containing about 100 eggs. They sink in the water..." THE BIOLOGY OF MAYFLIES, NEEDHAM, TRAVER, HSU, 1935.

It's odd that Epheron should have been first because it is not a common genus, and it is not true to form. For example, the wings of both species are translucent or milky white, not hyaline. The female does not molt into spinner, but mates, lays eggs and dies as a dun. The male changes to spinner soon after emerging, but must do it on the wing because its legs, except for the front ones, are so vestigal he cannot stand on them or hold onto anything long enough for the molt to take place. So, he molts in mid air, and sheds his "pellicle" which rains down to the surface of the river much like species of the Trichorythodes.

When I first heard about the Epheron species from Dan Gustafson, I became infatuated with them and couldn't wait to see my own live show. He had seen numerous emergences and males in the air flying with pellicles hanging from their bodies and wings.

I thought I had seen them, too, but not close and not clearly, on the lower Madison during the fall of 1984. They came mostly after dark and I fished an ancient soft hackle, the Grey Partridge, No 57, in Pritt's list, quite successfully, merely casting the fly to the noisy rises in the dark. Dave Kumlien of Montana Troutfitters knows of them and has fished and guided other anglers during their emergence. In 1994, he suggested I might find them in the late fall on the lower Jefferson or the lower Madison. Beginning around September 1, I made one trip to the Jefferson and four trips to the Madison from Bozeman waiting until way past darkness, ready to turn my car lights on if they appeared and scoop them up by the hundreds with just one sweep of my trusty, old net. One evening I saw a spectacular show of otters diving and splashing in the current; another of an unusual and stunning sunset from the smoke of the wildfires of the drought year; and another of criss-crossing flights of geese calling to one another in the darkness and my wondering how they could see enough of the dark land below them to put down or were they just going to keep flying nonstop to Idaho or Utah.

But no Epheron. No. Not until I talked to Tom Morgan, ex-guide and ex- owner of Winston Rods. "I used to see them on the ______," he said, "just about this time of year."

On September 25, my partner-wife and I drove to the

river and parked near a boat take-out . The river here runs into a wide, shallow flat and was showing its bones after a whole summer of constantly receding water. It was near 7 p.m., and I saw a whitish fly not too high off the water. Can it be? I ran back to the car for my boots and net and by the time I got back there were more. Hazel joined me on the bank. They were coming pretty good now, perhaps a dozen or so within easy reach, the oddly white wings making them easy to spot, where, with other spinners, you see only the bodies. Old workers' books said Epheron species stayed close to the water and didn't dance up and down like most spinners. It was true. They were not strong, evasive fliers and they were easier to net. Then a rare show among spinners; the actual mating in mid air and we both witnessed it.

With an 8x hand lens, I was able to check the color...or the lack of it...on the spot. My first impression was of a medium sized mayfly with smallish, black eyes and oversized, thick, white, translucent wings with purplish brown shading on the leading edges. The wings began well forward on the thorax and extended well back, more like a delta wing than the usual mayfly wing. The abdomen was white and nearly clear, with two tails. I knew I was looking at a male, because I noticed the long front legs, which, unlike the clear, and shrivelled up two other pairs, had what looked like meat and muscle in them. The only visible color was in the thorax, an almost pinkish, yellowy tan, which seemed to grow less pink, the older the specimen became. Females were the same color with three tails instead of two, same colored thorax and with all six legs clear and badly shrivelled. I began to photograph a female on a white dish when she started laying eggs. Yes, they were yellow. We returned to the spot at the same time on the next evening and saw only half as many albums as the night before. On the 27th, I returned with Tom Morgan and we saw only 5 or 6, one, a male which was trying to molt in my hand and which I tried to photograph. After three nights in a row with fewer and fewer insects, we reasoned we may have come upon them at the end of their mating cycle. Dan Gustafson verified the species without putting them under the microscope.

Measurements of one of the females as follows: tails, 1 and 1/8" long; body, 1/2" long; wing, 1/2". For fishing the fly in Montana, Pennsylvania, Michigan, New York, or wherever it may be found, I made quite a nice copy as follows:

Hook: Tiemco 109 BL, 15, painted white.
Abdomen: White danville, ribbed with fine gold wire and covered with fly tying cement or nail polish.
Thorax: Yellowy tan with a little pink mixed in..
Hackle: Largish white, squashed and halved flat after winding to look spent.
Tail: Three strands Lureflash.

Perhaps no mayfly symbolizes the short, ethereal life of the order with more sympathy than the Epheron. From MAYFLIES OF NORTH AND CENTRAL AMERICA, "The males patrol a short stretch of water. The emerging females join the males until mated, then immediately leave the swarm, settle on the water, expel their eggs, and die. Copulation lasts only a few seconds. After copulating, the males return to the swarms. Usually all members of a swarm are dead within an hour and a half after the start of the flight."

Green drake female spinners are rarely seen on some western rivers. Compare stocky abdomen to brown drake below. Brown drake spinners, are long and slender and easy to identify because of the brown clouds on the wings.

An L. cupida male regards his own exuvia. Note much longer front legs on the spinner than on the shuck. H. solitaria, below , with typical genus cross venation on front of wing. Darkening in tail can be male sperm.

Color is used less and less by workers to identify spinners. Horseshoe patterns on ventral side of abdomen of the gray drake (below) are still used to aid in naming the species.

An Epheron album escaping its exuvia on the water. Below, dying spinner. Females molt as duns. Males normally molt in mid air, cannot stand on their vestigal legs.

Male and female PMD's. Note much longer front legs on male, bigger eyes, slightly darker coloring in tail. Below. Male and female hopelessly entangled in their wing exuviae.

Among the smallest and largest spinners are the B. tricaudatus above and H. limbata below. Top-shaped eyes on B. and vitta on trailing edges of H. help identify both species

D. coloradensis, western green drake, above, shares hatches at times with the gray drake. Below: A late October PMD escapes its shuck while molting in author's living room.

The dun above and spinner below of the Callibaetis. The geometric pattern on the dun and vitta on the leading edge of the spinner are trademarks of the genus and species

T. hecuba, the so-called gray drake of Yellowstone Park, in late fall. Note parrallel longitudinal veins in front of the wings (below) which can be used in identifying. There is a Mount Timpanoga in northern Utah.

A male and female of a very small species, perhaps Baetis or Caenis from DePuys spring creek, look like art work. The H. solitaria below shows why it's difficult to design spinner bodies.

D. flavinlinea, dun and spinner above. I had poor luck capturing this species. Below is in question. Is this a Michigan Hendrickson, E. subvaria or L. cupida? Note deep, rich, brown abdomen.

P. bicornuta, (mahogany), male, showing exaggerated tails,and long front legs. Note nearly clear abdomen sections and claspers. Below is a Henry's Fork female who couldn't wait to get to the river.

Top clockwise: Baetis No. 1, Syl's Gold Plaited spinner, Caenis, Baetis No. 3.
Bottom clockwise: Callibaetis, Centroptilum, D. coloradensis, D. flavinlinea

Top clockwise: E. albertae, E. simulans, E. album, E. inermis.
Bottom clockwise: H. solitaria, L. cupida, P. bicornuta, R. futilis.

Top clockwise: R. morrisoni, R. robusta, S. occidentalis, R. undulata.
Bottom clockwise: S. quebecenis, S. vicarium, S. candensis, S. fuscum

Top clockwise: T. hecuba, Trico No. 1 (male), Trico No. 2 (female), Trico No. 3
Bottom: clockwise: D. grandis, H. limbata

# Heptagenia solitaria

## Stenonema vicarium, fuscum, and canadense

*(March Brown, Grey Fox, Light Cahill)*

I was very happy to find Heptagenia solitaria for this book because it is very similar to Stenonema which is a very important mayfly on classic eastern rivers. Both genera belong to the same family, Heptaginiidae. They both feature "typical Heptaginine venation" in the forewings which Gustafson describes as having "darker cross veins than longitudinal ones." They differ in size only, two of the Stenonema being a size or two larger than the Heptagenia.

It wasTom Travis, owner of Master Angler in Livingston, who steered me to the lower ____, in search of this mayfly. The date was October 9, 1994, a bit late to be finding a summer species, but not unusal for this drought year. "In Montana Heptagenia is a lower river critter, but because of lower flows and higher temperatures, it has made it up stream further and later than normal," says Gustafson.

My wife, Hazel, noticed the spinners while I was putting on waders on the river bank. It was sunny and warm, just after six. They were quite low over a shallow, rocky riffle, and because of that, we both thought they might be an Ephoron species. As I got closer, however, I saw their hyaline wings.

They were also a lot more wary and if I moved towards them, they moved away, but if I stood still, they would come to me and it would be a lot easier to net one or two.

I also discovered again that male spinners frequently make the mistake of flying to other males and actually touch them before they realize they could not mate. Male spinners, "not only fly up to females of other species, but at times are attracted to any fly of reasonable size which passes within a few feet of them. If an artificial Spent Gnat is tied on to a cast which is attached to a rod and line in the normal manner, and is then allowed to swing out in the wind near a swarm of male spinners, many of the spinners will fly over to it. The artificial fly becomes more attractive if it is drawn against the wind at about the speed at which a female spinner flies. The males then pursue it and knock against it, or even make abortive attempts to grasp it. But once they touch the artificial fly they lose interest, and return to the swarm." AN ANGLER'S ENTOMOLOGY, J. R. Harris.

The mating dance lasted for about an hour, during which time I actually saw a pair mating in the air. Later, I saw females laying eggs by skimming the water and dipping the tips of their abdomens into the surface, not all at once, but at certain intervals.

There were quite a few fish feeding on these spinners and I was anxious to try them with a new spinner pattern I had already made up in anticipation of findingthem. The fly was 5/16" long with three barbs of golden pheasant topping for a tail, a gold-ribbed, reddish brown body, light brown thorax and honey dun hackle, halved and spread out like the standard spinners in this book. There was a huge, shallow flat in the river and it was there I saw most of the rises. I was a bit suspicious of them; they didn't look like good, trout rises. I did not see any backs of fish, only the smallish circles, but I was anxious. Of course, they were all whitefish, but seven or eight of them took the new fly without hesitation. Tom told me later that the trout were up higher in the faster water.

At home, I measured and photographed the spinners: body and wing are 7/16" with prominent, black eyes on the males. Front legs on the male are fully as long as the body. There are two spotted tails, twice the length of the body. One of the specimens was a female with pale, yellow eggs starting to come out of the 7th or 8th segment. Wings are gorgeous with three wide, yellow, longitudinal veins at the front and thick, brown or black cross veins connecting the longitudinal ones. The venation, particularly the cross ones suggests stained glass, and, indeed, would make a rare and beatiful piece of art if it could be enlarged and framed and hung.

Color of the male and female are quite similar; an orangy, yellowy, mustardy sort of color with a see-through quality that's common among spinners. This see-through or hyaline quality is even more obvious on the Stenoma terminatum which is the only western species of that genus and which was collected by Gustafson on July 11, 1991 from the Smith River here in Montana. The species is smaller than solitaria, but you can read print through the middle segments. The head, thorax and last two segments are creamy yellow. The males have large, popping, black eyes and seem to have the longest fore legs and tails of any spinner I've seen. Wing venation is much the same as the solitaria.

There doesn't seem to be any material in the world which could imitate the solitaria sufficiently, but we'll take a stab at it with the following:

Hook: Tiemco 100, 14, painted white.
Body: Orange flymaster, ribbed with fine
gold wire, coated with wing coat or

fast-drying fly tying cement.
Thorax: Similar orange color as body.
Hackles: Honey dun or lightest
dun, and small, lightish partridge.

The two hackles are tied on to the hook shank simultaneously, chicken hackle behind the partridge. Wind hackle first, tie off, then one turn of partridge in front of the hackle. Turn vise towards you and divide and pinch the hackles in two. The addition of the partridge on this fly suggests somewhat the cross veining which characterizes the family and genus.

Without seeing any of the three eastern Stenonema species, but having at my disposal colored photos and descriptions, I'm suggesting the following patterns:

S. Vicarium (March Brown).
Hook: Tiemco 109 BL, 11.
Abdomen: Yellow, dabbed lightly with
brown marker, ribbed with gold
wire and coated with fly tying cement.
Thorax: Dark amber.
Hackle: Light dun and one turn of partridge,
divided and pinched in two halves.
Tail: Wood duck flank.

S. Fuscum (Grey Fox).
Hook: Tiemco 109 BL, 13.
Abdomen: Yellow dabbed with brown marker,
ribbed with gold wire and coated with
fly tying cement.
Thorax: Blackish brown.
Hackle: Light dun and one turn of partridge,

divided and pinched in two halves.
Tail: Wood duck flank.

S. Canadensis (Light Cahill).
Hook: Tiemco 109 BL, 15.
Abdomen: Yellow dubbed with brown marker.
Thorax: Darker brown.
Hackle: Light dun and one turn of partridge,
divided and pinched in two halves.
Tail: Golden pheasant topping feather.

To turn all of the previous patterns in this chapter into dun/spinners, merely replace hackles with medium dun and eliminate partridge.

## Hexagenia limbata, *(The Hex )*

## Leptophlebia cupida, Paraleptophlebia adoptiva

In May, 1994, I spent several days in Michigan and collected and studied some spinners which I found there. I could not easily identify the species here in Montana and sent them to Carl Richards who did so, for which I am grateful.

Carl identified two groups of these as Ephemera simulans (brown drake) which has a chapter to itself in the book. I found one group of Michigan simulans on Baldwin creek near Baldwin, which is the center of the fishing on the Pere Marquette, Little Manistee and other great trout waters of the state. This was from 1 to 3 p.m. on May 13, a nice, warm and sunny day. I was on a bridge over the river and saw the first of the spinners on the upstream side. They were quite low over the water, rising and falling no more than two or three feet. They were all males and seemed interested in anything that flew within sight, even darting quickly towards approaching caddis or other flying insects. The spinners may have been at this for a long time, because I actually saw one sit down on a twig sticking out of the water. He rested there for a few minutes, then got up and joined the small swarm. In flight, the spinners' abdomens were dark brown on the top and pale on the bottom, with quite a clear line running down the sides dividing the two shades of brown. This makes it difficult designing the imitation. Do you go with the lighter bottom side for the body which might be the side the trout sees first; or do you lean towards the darker brown top side which the angler sees first? It may not make a lot of difference, but there are least two ways to obtain somewhat of the two-toned effect, and I have listed them at the end of the chapter.

From Baldwin I proceeded north to the Little Manistee which I had not seen for quite a few years, and from 5 to 7 p.m., I saw and collected another group of spinners below the M37 bridge, part of which Carl also identified as Ephemera simulans. I have compared both groups with those from this area and they are the same mayfly, except the Michigan ones are at least one hook size larger.

There were some smaller spinners here which I also captured and which Carl identified as Paraleptophlebia adoptiva. The bicornuta of the same genus has been covered in another chapter. The females are identical in size and color so you can use the instructions from that chapter to tie this spinner imitation. These females put on quite a show of egg laying below the bridge which I had never seen before. They literally threw themselves into the river over and over, rising three or four feet between dives. One did it 8 times.

On May 14, I netted some largish, brown spinners with Mike Amboy on the Rogue in the city of Rockford, which Carl identified as Leptophlebia cupida. Mike called them Hendricksons immediately, and I was told by a fly shop and anglers to expect to see and collect Hendricksons because they were on the rivers.

But in most of the 'hatch' books the name, Hendrickson is given to Ephemerella subvaria, not a species of Leptophlebia. It's easy to see how the two species might be taken for one another. They show at about the same time, and they are about the same size and color. So here is my spinner dressing for the cupida and the subvaria:

Hook: Tiemco 109 BL, 11 or 13.
Body: Flymaster tobacco brown with
Orvis brown Flexi -Floss over.
Gold wire rib laid in the hollows
of the Flexi-Floss. Brownish black thorax,
tied heavy.
Hackle: Golden yellow. Honey dun or ginger.
Tail: Three long strands of golden pheasant
topping.

I found one other spinner on the Rogue river in Michigan which Carl identified as Siphlonurus quebecensis, or the gray drake. I have covered the occidentalis of that genus and suggest using the dressing given there.

Some of my readers may know that I fished a great deal in Michigan and that the first two books I authored on the soft-hackled fly were based mostly on angling experiences in that state. I never designed a soft hackle for the Hexagenia limbata, although I did fish the hatch whenever I could on the Manistee, S. Fork of the Au Sable, Pere Marquette and other trout streams. Fishing the Hexagenia is definitely a night time, near-pitch black experience. Of all the times I fished it, I can remember only once being able to see the water, the fly and the fish. About the time to start fishing was the saying: "...when you can count five stars in the sky..." or "...when you start to hear the whippoorwills singing..."

Perhaps it's just as well hex fishing is that way, otherwise there would be even greater addiction to it. Many hex anglers have caught the largest trout of their fishing lifetimes during the hatch. And others have lost their way in the darkness taking the 'shortcut' through a swamp to get to a certain productive spot on a river. One such angler I knew could not find his way out after a fabulous fishing evening and mounted a tussock and went to sleep until dawn. By the time he got out it was nine or ten in the morning by which time his wife reported him missing to the sheriff, who went out with a posse comitatus trying to find him.

I still have fishing friends in Michigan and one of them, Mike Caswell, sent me several of the 1994 crop of Hexagenia limbatas. The bodies are 1" long with wings about the same, possibly a little bigger. Two tails measure around 1-1/4" but there is also a stub of a tail in the middle of them.

The limbata presents the same problem to the fly designer as does the Ephemera simulans from the front of this chapter and many other spinners which have a darker top than bottom. On the limbata, the top of the thorax is dark purple and the bottom is olive tan, about the color of uncooked shrimp. On some existing deer hair fly patterns the two-tone effect has been accomplished with dark hair on top and light hair on the bottom. I suspect a woven body like George Grant's might provide the desired effect, but I cannot instruct you on that. One of the easiest methods is to build the body with thick, white thread, and coat the top of it with a purple or dark brown marker. Some of the color will run into the bottom side of the body giving it an on-and-off look, resembling the real thing.

The other suggestion is to use tying thread which matches the lighter, bottom color, and laying dark colored flexi-floss or thick yarn across the top of the fly and fastening it with the gold rib.

Here is the formal dressing for the Hexagenia limbata:

Hook: Tiemco 109 BL, 7.
Body: Heavy white thread, (at least 3/0),
with dark brown or purple marker
dabbed on top, ribbed with gold wire,
and coated with fly tying cement.
Heavy brown thorax.
Hackle: Badger (dark center) or grizzly.
Tail: 3 strands moose mane hairs.

# Paraleptophlebia bicornuta

*(Mahogany dun)*

In not many spinners does one find such a difference between the male and female, not only in size but also in coloring or shading, as in P. bicornuta, the subimago of which is called Mahogany dun. The male at 7/16" long is 1/8" bigger than the female. His abdomen, through the first three segments, is reddish brown then turns almost clear so that you could read through it if you had to, until the last two or three segments when they go reddish brown again. Some workers say the darker color in the last couple segments is a reflection of the sperm still left there.

There are three golden tails on both sexes and it was these tails which prompted me to try barbs of the golden pheasant topping feather on some of the spinners in this book.

The female, which we're going to imitate in this species, is not so difficult. She has a solid reddish brown abdomen and thorax which we can copy on a size 16 or 14 hook. Tobacco brown is the closest colored Danville thread for the body and we'll rib it with very fine gold rib, coat the body with fly tying cement, then dub a thorax of rusty brown and wind on a cock or hen hackle, preferably the white or dun with rusty edge or any light colored beige or ginger hackle.

This particular spinner also lends itself to the dyed or marker-painted peacock quill. If you use undyed quills, I would suggest the Sanford brown for the painting. Test the quill for strength after you have painted it to make sure it is strong enough to stand being wound on the hook. This saves swearing and aggravation. The quill is strongest, of course, towards the base and if it breaks in the testing, just keep working your way down until it resists breaking. You'll need only two inches or so of the quill which gives plenty of room to hold it between your thumb and forefinger. Tie in the small or thinner end and wrap the first turns gingerly and without a lot of pressure. Each wrap should be tight against the previous one. Depending on the width of the quill, you should get 8 or 9 wraps and end up around two thirds of the way towards the eye, on a 16. Now coat the wraps with fly tying cement, then add a smidgen of rusty brown dubbing, and finally tie in and wrap the hackle.

There is no need for a rib on spinners made with quills because the quill itself creates the segments as it is wound on the hook, which I feel is the purpose of the rib. Some of the photos in this book show those segments, but I would suggest using a small 8.0 power magnifying lens to check your work from time to time. Mine sits next to the vice for constant checking of fly construction and color. I also use it in the field when netting and photographing insects.

Species of Paraleptophlebia (apparently not the bicornuta) have been important mayflies of English fly fishers for many years, but it's hard to see why. At least two authors have said trout ignore the duns of turkey browns, the English nickname for the P. submarginata. I was netting bicornuta duns on a private spring creek near Bozeman when I noticed the same phenomenon. I was below a famous pool where 4 or 5 handsome residents of the creek almost always rise and I could clearly see the purply brown duns coming down. The trout rose steadily, some rising just inches from the mahogany duns but I never saw a trout take one. Is it the same taste of the Paraleptophlebia on two continents that keeps English and American trout from eating them, and might that resistance continue if that were the only food available to them?

Here is the formal dressing.

Hook: Tiemco 100, 16.
Body: Danville tobacco brown, ribbed with fine gold wire, coated with fly tying cement.
(Or stripped peacock quill, dyed or marker painted brown.)
Thorax: Dark brown.
Wing: Rusty edged hackle, split and flattened.
Tail: 3 barbs golden pheasant topping feather.

# Rithrogena morrisoni *(March Brown)*

## Rithrogena futilis, R. robusta and R. undulata

March Brown! Now that's a name to conjure. I already used it in the chapter on the Heptagenia as a synonym for S. vicarium and here I'm using it as a synonym for the R. morrisoni. In THE SOFT-HACKLED FLY, first published in 1975, there was a March Brown Spider. And before that in England there was the March Brown, an artificial of the natural fly, Rithrogena haarupi, which starts to appear in late March, April and early May. A DICTIONARY OF FLY-FISHING by C. B. McCully, says, "the fly is first mentioned in Chetham (The Angler's Vade Mecum, 1681), where it is called the Moorish Brown, and a further more detailed account of the fly is given in The Art of Angling by Richard Bowlker (1747), which gave a dressing not superseded for a hundred years. (Body: hare's fur ribbed with yellow silk; Hackle: partridge; Wings: pheasant or partridge)."

We can see the fly's fame is more firmly rooted as a nymph or a dun, but this is a book on spinners, and I saw and captured R. morrisoni spinners from the Yellowstone above Livingston, on April 26, 27, and 28, 1993 , and from April 29, 1994 , through May 5th of 1994; and from most of April and the early part of May of 1995.

The morrisoni is one of four Rithrogena species found in Montana. The others are futilis, robusta and undulata. All are spinners of medium to large size with brown or reddish brown bodies and wings with darker cross veins than longitudinal ones, typical of the Heptageniidae family. Though related, each species has its own preference for locale and time of appearance. As Gustafson tells us, the morrisoni is first to appear on relatively big water like the Yellowstone. The robusta is found in high mountain streams like Rock Creek in summer. At lower elevations, and also in summer are found the futilis and undulata on rivers like the Smith and Boulder.

The robusta, is the biggest of the four species with body and wings at 9/16" with two tails which are 1-1/4" long. Body is brown and very thin and streamlined. The morrisoni spinner is 7/16" long, the female being quite stocky in the orangy red body. The hyaline wing is also 7/16", with many short, dark veins crowded into the tips. The futilis has a 3/8" long orangy red body and wings the same length and similar characteristics. I have examined only male spinners of the undulata which were 5/16" in the body and wing, both hyaline except for the last two or three segments of the body.

I'm giving dressings for all four of these Montana Rithrogena species beginning with the morrisoni which is the species designated as the March Brown.

R. morrisoni

Hook: Tiemco 100: 14.
Abdomen: Orange with red marker.
Thorax: Dark brown.
Ribbing: Gold wire.
Hackle: Rusty edge.
Tail: Golden pheasant topping barbs.

R. futilis:

Hook: Tiemco 100: 16.
Abdomen: Reddish orange.
Ribbing: Gold wire.
Thorax: Reddish brown.
Hackle: Rusty edge or light dun.
Tail: Golden pheasant topping barbs.

R. robusta:

Hook: Tiemco 100: 12.
Abdomen: Brown.
Thorax: Dark brown.
Ribbing: Gold wire.
Hackle: Light ginger.
Tail: Golden pheasant topping barbs.

R. undulata:

Hook Tiemco 100: 16.
Abdomen: Coffee.
Thorax: Reddish brown.
Ribbing: Gold wire.
Hackle: Light ginger.
Tail: Golden pheasant topping barbs.

I was never much interested in fishing the morrisoni spinner on the Yellowstone, perhaps because its appearance coincided with the explosive Mother's Day Caddis. I did see quite a few morrisoni duns, however, along the banks of the river and I thought the duns could be well imitated with the dun/spinner style of fly suggested elsewhere in this book. I tied a pattern just like the morrisoni spinner above, except it had a lureflash tail and a dark dun hackle (not divided and flattened for wings and legs.) I couldn't tear myself away from the excellent caddis fishing, so I asked a friend, Fig Newton, if he wanted to try the fly for me, and he said yes. This was on April 30, 1994. He never moved from the inside curve of one of the big riffles on the river and caught 9 rainbows on the fly.

In 1995, I started fishing the Yellowstone on February 28, averaging three or four days a week. On April 3, I saw Baetis duns and on April 17, I saw the first morrisoni duns, which was the signal to start fishing spinners of that species.

So, taking the suggestion of Skues to fish spinners during a rise of duns, I fished the morrisoni spinner on May 2, on the same spot of water Newton fished nearly a year earlier. The weather was cold and the light was gray. I rarely was able to see the spinner in the quick moving riffle, but I saw the disturbance on the surface when the fish took and struck from impulse when I believed the trout had risen to the fly.

Not many fly fishermen would ever think of fishing spinners so early in the season, or when fish are feeding on duns. But on this day I had nearly 20 rainbows and cutts from a single riffle with the R. morrisoni spinner. I believe the thin silhouette of the body makes the fly more effective and I also think there is too much body--mostly from dubbing--on most dun and spinner patterns we fish today.

I never moved more than ten feet in one direction or the other during the two hours or so I fished this riffle. I had so many fish that I thought I was beginning to see a true cross -section of all the fish in that riffle. One nice sized cutt was missing a part of his bottom jaw, which had grown over into normal, healthy tissue. And another had a bad eye which apparently did not prevent him from seeing my morrisoni spinner.

# Timpanoga hecuba

Gustafson believes October is a good month for mayflies and spinners and based on this report on T. hecuba, you may agree. It begins in the Master Angler fly shop in Livingston in October, 1993, where the information board on the wall reported gray drakes "in the afternoon" on some of the eastern rivers in Yellowstone Park.

Gray drake is the fisherman's name for many species of the Siphlonurus family. Insects are quite large, (size 12 and 13), with purplish gray wings, two tails and a distinct horseshoe pattern on their abdomens.

The park at this time of the year is winding down. A fly shop in Gardiner agrees there is a gray drake hatch going on. Hundreds of elk wander the streets of Mammoth and park on the well-cared-for lawns. Once you leave Mammoth, you see few cars and few fishermen. The country looks bigger and more magnificent without much, except for small families of buffalo, moving around in it.

Only one section of the river is occupied with a guide and his two clients so it's easy for Hazel and I to find another. We settle on a big bend, fairly rapid with a good current throughout, the beginning of it marked by some bigger boulders which create a turbulent whitewater riffle. We carry rods and insect nets to the top of the bend and I tell myself if the gray drakes don't come, I'll fish.

It's often a good idea to sweep the banks of the river

with the net, hoping to find spinners from yesterday's or the day before's hatch of duns. No mayflies at all, no spinners, just some ants. So, I start to fish and make only a few casts when I see a 'gray drake' come down the river. It is huge, the purple gray wings giving the fly a topsy turvy look. The net is on the bank and it looks like I might just make it there and back and still catch the insect. I do and he goes into the special shoe box with a screened-in top.

Now, there are more, not dozens, but singles, one after another. The netting is easy standing in knee deep water and the shoe box starts to fill with the big duns.

I've worked my way up in the riffle and am near the top when I see some trout rise in the center of the fast water and on the slower edge. These are not sips, but big, fast whorls with flashes of orange and red. I have enough duns and hand the box to my wife, who hands me my fly rod.

For some time, I had been thinking of a dun/spinner fly with the body of the spinner and the wings of the dun. Such a fly would, if it worked, be very welcome in any angler's arsenal because he could fish it anytime as a dun or a spinner. For this occasion I made four of them on size 13 Tiemco 109 BL hooks, which are extra fine, extra long shank and barbless. Two of the flies were the same: Lureflash for tail, thin, tapering body of Danville tobacco brown, gold rib, rusty rabbit fur thorax and a large, dark blue dun hackle just wound around as the wings and the legs. The other two had the same bodies and thorax but white with rusty edge hackle and a couple strips of clear organza, the last sent to me by Gary Borger for trial.

I try the rusty-edged hackle fly first, casting upstream into the slower water along the edge where I saw a fish rise more than once. He takes the fly on the first cast and it turns out to be a fat cutthroat. Then another on the same fly in the fast water. Before it's over, I think I should try the other fly and I Turle it on the leader. It didn't seem to make any difference, light colored rusty edge or dark dun hackle, I took two more, the last of which was so big and strong, I hand the rod to my wife on the bank and she fights it for a while and lands it. I put the Winston 9 foot over the fish and eye ball its length from the back of the reel seat to the Winston cup insignia, which I find out later is just over twenty inches.

The 'gray drake' Gustafson tells me at the dissectiscope in his lab is not Siphlonurus but Timpanoga hecuba. It has three tails, not two, and it lacks the horseshoe markings on the abdomen which entomologists generally relate to the gray drake. Well, that's not the first time flies were called by the wrong name, and it certainly is easier to say gray drake.

Timpanoga hecuba is a subgenus of the genus Ephemerella. The dominant spinner body (abdomen) color is a shade of brown, with a darker thorax. The 10 segments are clearly distinguished with bands of gray. Body length is 7/16 to 1/2". Wing: 9/16", hyaline.

The spinner imitation is as follows:

Hook: Tiemco 109 BL: 13.
Body: Danville tobacco brown, ribbed with gray thread and gold ribbing, coated with fly tying cement.
Thorax: Rusty dubbing.
Wing: Rusty edged hackle and a couple strips of clear organza.
Tail: Three barbs golden pheasant topping feather.

# Tricorythodes minutus

From Hebgen Lake, a private spring creek near Bozeman, the East Gallatin, the Bighorn and other rivers in Montana, we have at least three different sized and three different colored spinners of the family Tricorythidae. In size they go from 1/8" to nearly 3/8". And even though they look black and are sometimes nick-named 'white-winged black', some of the smaller females have obvious dirty, yellow-orange abdomens, while the larger, Bighorn females have abdomens which are light green tapering to pale white or clear at segment number 8 or 9. Workers tell us females are often paler than males and we can confirm that. No matter what size and sex, trico spinners are short and stocky with pitch black thoraxes. The wings (no hind wings) are clear as glass, yet reflect a whitish cast under certain light conditions. The tails are perhaps the longest in proportion to body length of any spinners, 3 and 1/2 to 4 times.

What the insect lacks in size, it makes up for in quantity and availability. They come not as individual specimens but as whirlwinds, many feet in diameter and height. Males are said to emerge first from their nymphal shucks throughout the night, followed by the females beginning sometime after dawn. Molting into spinners ranges from almost immediate to up to two hours. The question of how the molt is accomplished, stationary or in flight, is in dispute. In my chapter on the final molt, I thought that one of the requisites for a successful molt of most mayflies was the necessity of the dun to grab on to something with its legs to keep it from sliding around while its back splits and the spinner works its way out of the shuck complete with new wings, head, eyes, legs, body, tails and mating equipment. I have witnessed that kind of trico molt many times on parts of my body, waders, automobiles, tables and buildings near certain rivers.

But many other anglers and I have also seen trico dun shucks fall out of the sky when a swarm of insects went over. This could have happened in two ways. The duns could have begun the molt in a stationary position and finished it off in mid air. Or the entire process began and ended in mid air. This is quite possible. Tricos are strong, fast fliers. Swarms have been documented a mile from any water and at heights of 100 feet or more. Powerful downward strokes of their wings could help cause the mesonotum to split. The head comes out followed by thorax, abdomen and legs, with the wings still flapping to hold the insect up. In the several actual mayfly molts I've seen, the wings and the tails come out last. If this is true with our flying trico, he could take a long sky dive with wings stationary and possibly pointed to the rear, finally freeing itself of the light, hollow, parachute-like, body and wings shuck trailing it.

After mating, females and males fall to the water in the hundreds of thousands. In some back eddies on larger rivers, spent tricos cover the water like a haze. This is primarily a morning activity, some workers having observed mating flights as early as 4:30. Some guides on the Bighorn take their clients out at daybreak. But, it takes a long time to sweep a river clear of millions of any kind of insect on the surface and I have enjoyed good trico fishing until one or two in the afternoon. Trico activity in Montana is also long-lived across the nicest weather we have, from the first of July through the middle or end of September.

There are a few special problems tying imitations of the spinners of Tricorythodes. The most obvious, of course, is the small size, although I don't believe they have to be tied as small as some writers have suggested. For at least 4 years, I have been fishing soft-hackled patterns on Tiemco 102 Y, size 19, which has a shank length of 3/16".

For most trico situations, I would stay with that size, but I would also tie some patterns on the Tiemco 900 BL, size 20 , which has a shank length of 1/8" and which is also barb free.

The question of the sex of the spinner is also a little problem. In most species, males ever or rarely, if ever, appear on the stream, I believe. In Tricorythodes, many spent males are to be found on the surface along with the females, and the trout obviously enjoy them as much as the females. The difference between the male and the female, as I have tried to point out, is in the abdomen, a shade of green or dirty yellow orange in some females, but black and white striped in the males.

Ribbing on size 20 hooks, laying down the base color in whatever material, then tying in and winding the rib is difficult, if not impossible. There just is not enough room. You can achieve the same effect very nicely, however, by tying in two Danville threads, black and white, or black and yellow or green and wind them up together to the thorax. For purer colored abdomens without ribbing, tie in some Danville orange or light olive and wind it up to the thorax where we tie in a strand or two of meaty peacock. It's quite amazing that this very common and cheap material actually helps to float the fly, besides giving the appearance of the thick, black thorax so prevalent on all tricos, male and female. The fly is finished with three or four turns of a white cock or hen hackle, split, divided and formed into two halves with wet or waxed thumbs and forefingers.

It's on a small fly like this that the thread body idea put forth in this book (and in some classic literature before it) manifests itself convincingly.

Here are the dressings in tabulated forms.

Trico No. 1. Male:
Hook: Tiemco 102 Y, 19 or Tiemco 900 BL, 20.
Body: Black & light olive Danville thread wound together to just past the center of the hook.
Thorax: Meaty, single strand of peacock.
Wings: White hackle, divided in two and formed.
Tail: Three micro fibbetts left long.

Trico No. 2. Female:
Hook: Same.
Abdomen: Light olive.
Thorax: Peacock.
Ribbing: None.
Hackle: White.
Tail: Micro fibbetts.

Trico #3:
Hook: Same.
Abdomen: Black and light olive.
Thorax: Peacock.
Ribbing: None.
Hackle: Grizzly.

Tail: Micro fibbetts.

(Note: I discovered from the two trico spinner patterns in SOFT-HACKLED FLY IMITATIONS that the white winged pattern is more easily seen against any bank foliage; and that the grizzly winged pattern is more easily seen in the glare of the center of the river.)

# Doubles

There doesn't seem to have been much work or thinking done along the idea of 'doubles', two small flies tied on one bigger hook, when trying to imitate small naturals like tricos, sulphurs and Baetis until the publication of MICROPATTERNS by Darrel Martin in 1994. Martin calls them "Knotted Patterns" in this wonderful book, and points out that "three-fourths to nine-tenths of all insects are less than 6.5 millimeters long." (Doubles are not to be confused with the British 'wee doubles', small flies with double bends, points and barbs.)

We certainly don't like to fish 20's, 22's and 24's, but there are times when those are the only sizes that will work on big, steadily feeding trout. Doubles make the game only a little easier than fishing the single micropattern, but furnish the satisfaction of 'small fly/big fish' just the same.

The first double I ever saw was on the Big Horn, in 1993. Bill Finney from State College, Pa, showed it to me and he claimed it worked quite well during the September trico hatches. It was tied on a size 16 with two sets of black bodies and two sets of poly yarn wings, one set behind the other. In Martin's book, the wings are tied further apart at the front and over the bend of the hook as on the famous 'fore and aft' Renegade or House And Lot patterns.

My first thinking about doubles, was, of course, for trico spinners. I saw them by the jillions on different waters, where frequently there could be as many as 10 or 15 in one square inch, many of them touching each other. I don't believe they fell on the river that way, but it was more the wave or current action which clumped them together on the surface, specially in lees and eddys. I do believe, however, it's possible for a mating pair of tricos or other mayfly spinners to be blown down to the water's surface accidentally.

In netting other kinds of spinners during the last couple of years, I frequently saw other mayfly spinners close enough together (not, however, like tricos) to make me think doubles of baetis, sulphurs and other micro-sized spinners might be feasable. And on October 13, 1994, at the Blue Gate of DePuy spring creek, Lars Olson, a guide, and I made an assault on the trout of that famous creek armed with some new spinner doubles. There had been tremendous hatches of Baetis tricaudatus, one just a few days before which mystified Lars and his client, and just about every other angler on the spring creek. Lars was looking for revenge and was eager to guinea pig these new flies with me. They were tied on 16 and 18 Tiemco 100 hooks with yellow, orange and red bodies, gold ribs and dun and honey dun hackles.

Lars started with the orange body just below the Blue Gate bridge and hooked and landed a fish immediately. He lost the fly trying to remove it from the trout and replaced it with a yellow. By this time I was fishing too, but now, mixed in with the tiny Baetis, was another larger, (16), yellowy green fly which the trout were starting to take along with the smaller Baetis, and milking down their concentration on the smaller fly. But why were they so late in the year? You guessed it, PMD, another quirk effect of the drought year.

Before we quit, Lars caught three fish on his double spinner patterns, and I also hooked three but never landed a single one. Since then I've had the opportunity to net other

Baetis tricaudatus duns in connection with this book, and noticed several times that even when the hatch is not too heavy, the duns seemed to like being close to each other coming down the river and that, on occasion, I saw one dun leave the water, fly and settle close to another a short distance away, as though he was looking for company.

So, why not a dun double along with the spinner double?

First, the dun double for Baetis tricaudatis:

Hook: Tiemco 100: 16.
Bodies: Two sets dark green olive dubbing, one behind the other. (Alter body dubbings to match the hatch.)
Wings: Medium dun hackles, barbs stripped off one side for slimness and neatness.
Tail: Three or four strands of clear Lureflash.

Spinner doubles:

Hook: Tiemco 100, 16.
Bodies: Two sets yellow Flymaster tapered bodies, one behind the other. (Alter to match other spinner bodies.)
Ribbing: Fine gold wire.
Wings: Light ginger or honey dun hackles, barbs stripped off one side for slimness and neatness.
Tail: Three micro fibbetts or wood duck flank feathers.

## Tying Spinners

Remember Halford's prediction in the chapter on the history of spinners, that quill, gut and hair for bodies will have been abandoned in favor of dubbing? I think we can all agree that in the year 1995, when this book was published, this is true. Natural or artificial, dubbing is now available in just about any color or shade imaginable. It's easy to get and easy to use. Wax the thread and spin a little dubbing on with your thumb and forefinger and 'voila,' you've got yourself a pretty good body for duns, caddis and stoneflies, but not for spinners.

Dubbing for spinners is too hairy and too thick. Look at the bodies of spinners (there are plenty of them in this book) and what do you see? You see a smooth, glowing, luminous, and thin body, clearly segmented into the 10 joints of the abdomen. In some spinners, Timpanoga hecuba and Ephemerella inermis, for example, the bodies or parts of them, are transparent.

In certain Paraleptophlebia species, certain joints appear to be metallic and highly polished, like silver or gold. Spinner bodies, are reflective, not absorbent, and to my way of thinking, dubbing is absorbent. (Halford didn't like it because it absorbed water and was difficult to dry in the false casting.) Dubbing is too thick. Let me throw some spinner dimensions at you so you can see what we're up against. These are from a female spinner E. inermis or Pale Morning dun. The diameters of the second segment from the thorax is .028 and from the ninth segment near the tail is .018, a difference of .010 from top to bottom. (It was easier to measure those two joints rather than number one and number ten.) The length of the spinner is approximately 5 / 16" which would indicate a size 16, if we were going to make a copy. Now, let's get diameters of the hook and materials we would use for the imitation including dubbing and put them in a table. Bear in mind these figures are approximate. (The Tiemco 5230 was the smallest diameter hook I could find. The shanks of most designated dry fly hooks in size 16 are .014 to .016 in diameter.)

| | |
|---|---|
| Tiemco 5230 3XF, size 16 | .012 |
| Flymaster tying thread | .002 |
| Any average tail material and gold wire ribbing | .004 |
| Dubbing (Fly-rite #18 dubbed as fine as possible on Flymaster tying thread) | .006 |
| Total | .024 |

With the dubbing method, we are .006 over the diameter of the tail end of the natural, but if we used just the tying thread, we could save .004, and get within just .003 of the real thing. Of course, on larger sizes, a thread body eliminates all the problems of thickness, and on smaller sizes, 18's and 20's, we could replace the gold ribbing with tying thread to save a couple thousands if we wanted to. I tried many ways to find the 'right' kind of body for the spinners in this book including floss, Larva Lace, Swannundaze, Flexi-Floss, various natural and artificial dubbings, goose biots and others, but found that most of them created a body which was too thick. I particularly liked the Orvis Flexi-Floss because it has a 'squishy', segmented, liquid look. It might work on a 14 and bigger hook, but in this book, we use it on some larger bodies to build them up quicker.

**T**ying Thread

There are many brands and kinds of tying threads, and I have settled on Danville flymaster which is available in many fly shops, comes in 14 colors, lies flat and has a nice, reflective sheen. There are other, finer tying threads, but they seem coarse and rough and less reflective. To obtain that glistening finish or luminousity spinners seem to have, I coat the body with a fly tying cement which dries fast enough to finish the fly at one sitting. Various fast drying nail polishes can also be used. (Marvin Nolte's patterns in the photographs were coated with nail polish.)

There are at least a couple colors of spinner bodies which cannot be matched by the existing Danville colors. And there are other bodies which have nearly clear segments in the middle of their abdomens. For these, I'm suggesting painting the shanks white, then forming the body with white tying thread and painting the ends with the right colored markers. This is the only way to get this kind of two-toned body without cutting off one colored thread, adding another, cutting it off and adding still another and cutting it off, all of which adds unwanted bulk to the body of the fly.

That's one body style. Really quite simple, but not without precedent as we have seen in the chapter on the history of spinners in fly tying.

## Stripped, Dyed Peacock Quills

As we have seen, stripped and dyed peacock quills were used for bodies of mayfly duns and spinners for at least 300 years. Until about 20 years ago, one could buy them in many different colors, packaged and ready to use. Why did they go out of favor?

Well, they are troublesome to strip and dye and work with, and one might conjecture dubbing took over or quills went the way of commercial fly tying in America...out of it! But there is no other material, natural or synthetic, which gives such a thin, realistic spinner body and we're going to use them even if we have to dye them ourselves.

An article by A. K. Best in the March 1991 FLY ROD AND REEL describes the method for stripping and dyeing hackle quills, which is almost the same as peacock quills. Before we start, I would suggest a trip to a Salvation Army or Goodwill store where you should buy your own pan or two for the process. Then, mix two cups of hot tap water with 1/2 cup of laundry bleach in a pan and soak a peacock eye or eyes, 6 to 10 inches, in it to remove or 'burn' off the flue. Agitate the eye in the mixture gently and the flue will begin to fall off the barbs immediately and form a scum. Leave the eyes in the bleach mixture just long enough to burn off all the flue, then remove them quickly. Dump the bleach mixture and wash in cold, running water for 5 minutes.

In two cups of warm water add a palmful of hair conditioner and soak the eyes in it for five minutes. (The bleach mixture dries out the natural oils and the hair conditioner tends to put some back.) Now rinse the eyes in cold, running water for five minutes and air dry on newspapers, making sure the barbs are separated from each other. Dye them the color you prefer in either a dye made for fly tying,

(Veniard) or Rit, a household product available anywhere.

You can eliminate the dyeing process entirely by taking individual barbs off the eye and 'painting' them with broad tip colored markers, such as Design 2, made by Eberhard Faber, Berol Prismacolor and Sanford HI IMPACT. The first two brands come in all the primary colors as well as blends, while the Sanford is available only in 8 primary colors. I would suggest, a dark red, orange, brown, olive or light green, yellow, tan or beige and black. To 'paint' a barb, just place it, thick end first, on the edge of a piece of cardboard, press the broad tip on the barb and pull it to the end. Wait a second and turn the barb over and do it again on the other side. The flueless barbs accept the darker, marker colors quite well, but not so well in the very pale white, cream or yellow tints. For these, I suggest tying the bodies with white, yellow, eggshell, beige or maize Flymaster tying thread, and painting the hook shanks white before starting.

### Stripped, Dyed Hackle Stems

D's Flyes has come out with 11 colors of stripped and dyed hackle stems which make nice bodies on these new spinners. The stems have to be soaked in water prior to tying. The company address is D's Flyes, 1999 So. Zenobia St., Denver, CO, 80219, 303 934 7066.

### Dyed Moose Mane Quills

I owe the suggestion of using moose mane quills for bodies of spinners to Ed Thomas. He used two barbs of contrasting shades, turned thick end to thin, which produced a nice, natural segmented body for a mosquito pattern he ties. I began to look for the whitest and longest-barbed piece of moose mane I could find at Dan Bailey's in Livingston with the idea that I would dye them and try them on some of the new spinner patterns in this book.

Surprisingly, moose mane barbs take dyes nicely, have a nice gloss and can be wound on a hook shank without breaking as often as peacock quills or hackle stems. Individual stems or barbs are quite 'slippery' and do not accept marker colors as well as tying thread. Individual dyed barbs can be wound on the hook shank then ribbed with gold wire, or they can be doubled, dark color and light, and wound on together for a ribbed effect without the gold rib.

**Tails**

The first is two or three barbs of a golden pheasant topping feather, which as you know, is the classic tail and wing material for many Atlantic salmon patterns. The barbs are yellow gold in color and have a reflective glint which seems to give off light resembling many of the tails on the darker bodied spinners. There is also a natural, jaunty curve upward in the barbs which you must try to maintain when tying them in at the tail. One way to do this is to lay the barbs on a dark surface and move them around until they are all facing the same way, then picking them up with thumb and forefinger and tying them in at the tail. A small drop of fly tying cement on the thicker stubs also helps hold the barbs together. (In salmon flies, a whole feather with many barbs is generally used. Here, we are stripping three or four individual barbs off the whole feather and tying them in at the tail.)

The second kind of tail is two or three barbs of a wood duck flank feather. After looking at quite a few spinners through small powered lenses and through a microscope, I began to notice that many tails were spotted. This feather, without the band, has a nice, lemony cast to it. Tie these barbs on the hook with the natural curve upward.

Three or four strands of clear Lureflash can be used on any of the dun/spinner patterns, and is suggested for the Epheron album, the white fly. You may want to use three or four moose mane barbs for the very large flies like the Hex, Green Drake or Brown drake, and, of course, I have suggested micro fibbetts for some patterns of the trico.

Whichever tail you prefer for spinners, make sure you tie them long enough. Spinner tails are unbelievably long and have never appeared long enough on artificial patterns to match the real thing. Twice the length of the hook shank should be the minimum length, with some patterns calling for three and four times the length of the body.

## Wings

Designing and installing wings on spinners has been the bane of fly tyers since fly tying began. There is virtually no color or substance to them except some dark spots on the leading edges of certain of the Callibaetis tribe. Spinner wings are veined and transparent, yet they seem to give off color points and lines which are never defineable and reproducible. From this, it might seem clear that the suggested wing is better than the specific one, ie, a hackle only, (no hackle points, no sections of a wing quill and no poly yarn), wound at the thorax of the fly; or wound in the same place, but then split and flattened somewhat to become what Marinaro and Woolley called hackle fibre wings.

Earlier, I promised to give their instructions on how to do this, and here they are. We'll start, non-verbatim, with Marinaro from IN THE RING OF THE RISE. The hackle is wound around the hook five or six times in turns next to each other, the rest of the turns splitting the previous turns in two. Now, the tying thread is used in figure 8's on top of and under the hackles to split and elevate the fibers, half on one side of the hook and half on the other.

Woolley's instructions are slightly different. He calls for far fewer turns and suggests figure eights on top of the hook, then turning it over in the vice and using figure eights to separate the hackle fibers from that position, which I found easier than Marinaro.

My method of splitting the hackle into a full spent spinner position is much the same, except I have discovered that the barbs can be 'bent' rather permanently into position by dividing, bunching and pulling or stroking them with slightly waxed or wetted thumbs and forefingers. This method needs no figure eights and is surprisingly easy to perform. I have suggested various hackles for the 30 patterns in the book and they can be cock or hen. The cock hackle will undoubtedly help to keep the fly higher in the film. However, my preference is for hen hackles because they are finer in texture and seem to offer more of the colors I prefer.

Some writers have suggested tying spinner wings with a full hackle for greater visibility. I have not seen spinners on the water in any other position but fully spent except for a few Callibaetis females. Wing muscles form the largest group on a mayfly and are, naturally, the first to fail after copulation in mid air and laying fertilized eggs on the water. The insect just cannot hold its wings up.

I also believe there is no reason for males to end up on the water (except for fast molting Caenis or Tricorythodes) unless they accidentally fall on it during or immediately after copulation, although imitations of male spinners have been designed and written about. And many workers believe that certain male spin ners return to a 'flight' or 'dance of males' in order to copulate with another female. How many times a male can do this we do not know.

Those are the special, fly tying instructions pertaining to all of the spinners found in this book. Dressings for all 30 patterns are included on the following pages. Tails are abbreviated: GPTF for golden pheasant topping feather and WDF for wood duck flank feather.

Baetis No. 1:

Hook: Tiemco 100: 16, 18
Abdomen: Unithread, rusty brown
Thorax: Reddish brown
Ribbing: Gold wire
Hackle: Rusty or ginger
Tail: WDF

Baetis No. 2. Syl's Gold Plated Spinner:

Hook: Tiemco 100: 16, 18
Abdomen: Yellow
Thorax: Light brown
Ribbing: Gold wire, close or solid wraps
Hackle: Rusty or ginger
Tail: WDF

Baetis No. 3:

Hook: Tiemco 100: 16, 18
Abdomen: Yellow Danville

Thorax: Pinky tan
Ribbing: Gold wire
Hackle: Rusty or ginger
Tail: WDF

Caenis:

Hook: Tiemco 100: 20 painted white
Abdomen: Eggshell
Thorax: Light brown plus pink
Ribbing: Gold wire
Hackle: White or rusty
Tail: GPTF

Callibaetis:

Hook: Tiemco 100: 16
Abdomen: Gray
Thorax: Reddish brown
Ribbing: Copper wire
Hackle: White or rusty with partridge in front
Tail: WDF

Centroptilum (Yellow sulphur):

Hook: Tiemco 100: 20 painted white
Abdomen: Yellow
Thorax: Pink
Ribbing: Gold wire
Hackle: Off white
Tail: GPTF

D. coloradensis (W. green drake):

Hook: Tiemco 109 BL: 13
Abdomen: Light olive
Thorax: Dark olive
Ribbing: Gold wire
Hackle: Rusty plus organza in front
Tail: GPTF

D. flavinlinea (Flav):

Hook: Tiemco 100: 16
Abdomen: Coffee
Thorax: Brown
Ribbing: Gold wire
Hackle: Organza
Tail: GPTF

D. Grandis (Green Drake):

Hook: Tiemco 109 BL: 11
Abdomen: Olive plus green Flexi-Floss
Thorax: Dark brown
Ribbing: Medium gold wire
Hackle: Off white or ginger
Tail: GPTF or moose mane

Epeorus albertae:

Hook: Tiemco 100: 16 painted white
Abdomen: Eggshell
Thorax: Light tan
Ribbing: Gold wire

Hackle: Rusty or light ginger
Tail: WDF

Ephemera simulans (Brown drake):

Hook: Tiemco 109 BL: 11
Abdomen: Brown plus brown Flexi-Floss
Thorax: Reddish brown
Ribbing: Mediuim gold wire
Hackle: rusty or light ginger
Tail: WDF

Ephemerella inermis (PMD):

Hook: Tiemco 100: 16 painted white
Abdomen: Light olive
Thorax: Pale yellow
Ribbing: Gold wire
Hackle: Rusty or reddish ginger
Tail: GPTF

Epheron album (White fly):

Hook: Tiemco 109 BL: 15 painted white
Abdomen: White
Thorax: Pinkish tan
Ribbing: Gold wire
Hackle: White
Tail: Clear lureflash

Heptagenia solitaria:

Hook: Tiemco 100: 14 painted white
Abdomen: Orange
Thorax: Darker orange
Ribbing: Gold wire
Hackle: rusty
Tail: GPTF

Hexagenia limbata:

Hook: Tiemco 109 BL: 7
Abdomen: Brown
Thorax: Dark brown
Ribbing: Large gold
Hackle: Badger or grizzly
Tail: Moose mane

Leptophlebia cupida:

Hook: Tiemco 103 BL: 13
Abdomen: Brown
Thorax: Dark brown
Ribbing: Gold wire
Hackle: Rusty or ginger
Tail: WDF

Paraleptophlebia bicornuta (Mahogany dun):

Hook: Tiemco 100: 16
Abdomen: Brown
Thorax: Dark brown
Ribbing: Gold wire

Rithrogenia futilis:

Hook: TMC: 16
Abdomen: Reddish orange
Thorax: Reddish brown
Ribbing: Gold wire
Hackle: Light dun
Tail: GPTF

Rithrogenia morrisoni (March brown):

Hook: TMC: 14
Abdomen: Orange dabbed with red marker
Thorax: Dark brown
Ribbing: Gold wire
Hackle: Dun
Tail: GPTF

Rithrogenia robusta:

Hook: TMC 100: 12
Abdomen: Brown
Thorax: Dark brown
Ribbing: Gold wire
Hackle: Ginger
Tail: GPTF

Rithrogenia undulata:

Hook: Tiemco 100: 16
Abdomen: Coffee
Thorax: Reddish brown
Ribbing: Gold wire
Hackle: Ginger
Tail: GPTF

Siphlonurus occidentalis (Gray drake):

Hook: Tiemco 109 BL: 13
Abdomen: Coffee
Thorax: Reddish brown
Ribbing: Gold wire
Hackle: Rusty plus organza
Tail: GPTF

Siphlunorus quebecenis (Gray drake):

Hook: Tiemco 109 BL 13
Abdomen: Coffee
Thorax: Medium brown
Ribbing: Gold wire
Hackle: Rusty plus organza
Tail: WDF

Stenonema vicarium (March brown):

Hook: Tiemco 109 BL: 11
Abdomen: Yellow, dabbed with brown marker

Thorax: Dark amber
Ribbing: Gold wire
Hackle: Honey dun plus partridge
Tail: WDF

Stenonema fuscum (Gray fox):

Hook: Tiemco 109 BL: 13
Abdomen: Yellow, dabbed with brown marker
Thorax: Dark amber
Ribbing: Gold wire
Hackle: Honey dun plus partridge
Tail: WDF

Stenonema canadensis (Light Cahill):

Hook: Tiemco 109 BL:15
Abdomen: Yellow, dabbed with brown marker
Thorax: Dark amber
Ribbing: Gold wire
Hackle: Honey dun plus partridge
Tail: WDF

Timpanoga hecuba:

Hook: Tiemco 109 BL: 13
Abdomen: Coffee
Thorax: Rusty
Ribbing: Gold plus gray thread
Hackle: Off white
Tail: GPTF

Trico No. 1 (Male):

Hook: Tiemco 102 Y: 19 or 902 BL: 20
Abdomen: Black and light olive
Thorax: Peacock
Ribbing: None
Hackle: White
Tail: Micro fibbetts

Trico No. 2 (Female):

Hook: Tiemco 102 Y: 19 or 902 BL: 20
Abdomen: light olive
Thorax: Peacock
Ribbing: None
Hackle: Grizzly
Tail: Micro fibbets

Trico No. 3:

Hook: Tiemco 102 Y: 19 or 902 BL: 20
Abdomen: Black and light olive
Thorax: Peacock
Ribbing: Fine gold wire like Lagartun
Hackle: Grizzly
Tail: Micro fibbetts

# Fishing Spinners

Drag, not fishing downstream, said Halford, is the no-no in dry fly fishing. It's on page 124 of his first book, FLOATING FLIES AND HOW TO DRESS THEM, 1886. I'll save you the looking. "Where it is impracticable to throw up stream, cast across and slightly up, and where this is impossible, cast directly across, and lower the hand slowly as the fly floats down, so as not to drag it.

"...Occasionally, however, it is impossible, either owing to natural obstructions on the bank or other causes, to fish a spot excepting by casting directly, or nearly directly, down stream;..." I beg the readers' pardon for quoting this twice, in my last book, SOFT-HACKLED FLY IMITATIONS as well as here, but these are the first and best instructions I know of for the 'modern' method of dry fly fishing, down stream reach casting. There is a little difference, however. We don't wait for 'natural obstructions'. We just do it all the time because it's easier and has the advantage of not lining the fish. It permits heavier tippets, too, because the trout sees the fly first. And it's easier because there is time and room to correct the position of the fly before it gets to the trout. Halford never said the fly has to float drag free all the time!

Fishing any small spinner without drag, either upstream or down is perhaps the most difficult kind of fly fishing. You must have good vision and there must be that kind of light from the sky which helps to illuminate the fly. In the dusk when spinner fishing is most practiced, that kind of light is hard to find. You must also work constantly to prevent drag by taking up line if you're fishing upstream and letting it out if you're fishing down with a reach cast.

So, I'm suggesting downstream reach casting with the spinner patterns in this book without drag most of the time, and, believe it or not, with drag under certain conditions.

## Drag Free

Try to position yourself approximately 45 degrees above the trout. When you see a rise, fix the spot in your mind and wait for the repeat. Most of the time, the trout will rise in exactly the same spot. He has already done his math and physics and he is convinced he has the best spot in the river for a continuous supply of those juicy morsels.

Pull three or four good sized loops of line off the reel and an additional amount which will be the casting portion. Cast at least three feet above the trout and slightly beyond it to give you room to adjust the fly by pulling it across the surface in line with him, before it reaches the trout. (That's one of the reasons for the excess loops hanging from your reel. The manuever also helps to straighten the leader guaranteeing more positive takes.) You also want the fly to pass the trout's feeding position on the inside of your side of him. In this way, you see him better when he rises to the fly because he's turning toward you. If the target trout does not take the fly, but there are others feeding below him, feed one or more of the excess loops into the cast to keep on fishing.

If you have been fishing dry fly for a long time with size 12 and 14 Royal Coachmans, Adamses, Wulff hair-winged flies or other similar 'dry' flies, you will not take lightly to fishing the spinners in this book. First, forget about seeing the fly, and learn how to judge where the fly is by watching where it enters the water. That is the most critical part, because if you can see where it goes in you should be able to know when a trout takes the fly even if you can't see it.

If you must, slam the fly into the water so you can see the disturbance and entry. Greasing the last two feet of the leader also helps. And never change the length of the leader. Whatever length you use, 9 foot, 11 foot, 13 foot, stay with it. And if you have to change flies often, then add tippet to make up for the shortening. Remember, most trout do not move too far from their feeding posts, so if you think your fly is in his vicinity and you see him rise, just tighten and chances are you'll have him. This is a little tougher than keeping your eyes glued to your regular kind of dry fly but this kind of fishing is the mark of a superior angler and you'll feel better because you've just expanded your dry fly fishing capabilities by100 percent.

## Drag

In the course of many hours of fishing spinners and fishing them on different kinds of trout waters, you will invariably come to the time and place when you can only fish the fly with drag because the trout is so far away and/ or it'll be so dark you won't be able to see the fly. Don't shudder, but be prepared for some extra jolts of adrenalin, like this occasion on the Big Horn in May 1993. Four of us had floated from Three mile to Thirteen mile and had pretty good fishing all the way down. Now it was seven and we were just coasting with the current because the takeout was still three miles away. Someone noticed fish rising on the left bank on the inside of a large, slightly curved riffle and we pulled over and got out of the raft. The trout were in a frenzy, but wading out as far as we could, most of them were just barely reachable with a fifty or sixty foot cast.

I had been fishing a rusty spinner, Lureflash tail, rusty dubbing and white with rusty edge hen hackle. On my first or second cast, a brown nearly pulled the rod out of my hand, even though I could not see the fly nor could I make any effective mends to correct for drag. Earl Dorsey quickly appeared at my side.

"What did you take him on?"

"Rusty spinner, dragging. "

"Give me one."

I opened a box and gave him one, and looking down on the on the water we both saw the water covered with the lobster-red bodied spinners.

Dorsey returned to the head of the riffle and started hooking the rising trout on the swing. Another friend, Jean Paul Samba, who I met earlier in Monaco and was able to join us on this trip, came over to get his rusty spinner, and he, too, started hooking the frenzied fish. We were all in the same boat; long casts with no control, dwindling light and trout going mad.

We missed a larger percentage because we couldn't see the take, but felt the savage pulls anyway.

Then, on Sept 23, 1994, the same kind of thing happened again, with more intention than previously. This time, I was with Dean Yannias on the Yellowstone out of the park. He was on the east side of the river and I was on the west. He was doing quite well with some kind of dry fly. I rigged up a two fly cast, just as I had been doing for more than 40 years with soft-hackled flies. On the dropper I tied a Mother's day caddis (peacock body, partridge hackle with all the barbs pulled up on top of the hook and a largish head made of mole fur.) On the tail, I tied on one of my new medium-sized spinners with a brown tying thread body, gold rib, dark brown thorax, long tail from the golden pheasant topping feather, and rusty edge hackle, divided and flattened as per the instructions in this book.

There were no trout rising so it was just going to be blind fishing the water with swinging or dragging flies. I made a few casts, the flies reaching the region in the big river where the slow water met the fast. I stepped a foot downstream between every cast. There was a monstrous pull and in the vicinity of the two flies I saw a great turbulence. Then the line started going down stream, pulling itself off the reel. Yannias, on the other side of the river, watched. I was nearly out of line, when the pulling lessened. There was still something pulling on the line, but no where near the pull which took all the line and nearly all of the backing out a few moments before.

I reeled up and found a 12 or 13 inch rainbow on the dropper, but the three feet of leader to the spinner, the tail fly was gone. So I had two fish on simultaneously and unfortunately lost the bigger one.

Toward the end of the 1994 season, I fished the new spinners more often without a dropper, in exactly the same way on big rivers, with reasonable success when nothing else was showing. The design of the fly is clean with no rigid protuberances so the fly shows little alarming disturbance when swung.

## The Evening Rise

The evening rise is everything to the British, far more

to them than it ever was to us. Perhaps it was "tea" which came luckily at just the right time, during the lull when all the afternoon fishing seemed to be coming to a close, and the evening rise had not yet begun.

John Waller Hills writes of the value of the evening rise in A SUMMER ON THE TEST, 1924. He divides it into three parts, the first, the 'casual' rise between 6 and 7 p.m.; the second, the 'small fly rise', beginning when the "last edge of the sun has sunk below the actual horizon and ends when it is too dark to see a small artificial on the water." The third rise, in what must be nearly total darkness, lasts for "something under half an hour, rarely longer." In England that could take you to nearly 11 p.m. because of its more northern latitude.

Hills suggests the sherry, the orange, and the red spinners for most of the fishing in the first two stages, but switches to a large sedge, or caddis, for the last and darkest part of the rise.

The Montana evening rise is more like this. The duns which have been on most of the day begin to thin out and there's a half hour or so without much happening. There is an unwholesome glare on the water as though it had lost all of its transparency. Fish stop feeding. The sun continues its downward climb and suddenly there is a nice, warm, rosy glow everywhere you look. Water in the shallows over rocks and weeds looks like ribbons. It's hard to take your eyes off them. Now, fresh looking duns, lighter in color than before, may appear on the water again, the same species as before or a different species.

Look down on the surface now and you may see spinners, flush with the surface. They leave no shadow, so you must look straight down to see them. They are mostly Hill's colors: orange, red, brown, rusty or reddish brown bodies, and it will be time to fish a spinner in any of these colors. These are the body colors which I believe are heightened or glorified by the last rays of the sun. Fish the spinner to trout you see rising to the remaining duns. The trout have seen and fed on the spinners long before you saw them. They're ready for you.

It can happen that way or this. The duns are no more, but the trout start to go mad, rising to something you can't see. You think it's midges. Your dun or generic dry fly stops working, yet you go on throwing it out there in desperation. Float after drag-free float. Trout rise inches from your fly. You grow more desperate, and somewhere in the pit of your stomach you realize you're not the fly fisherman you thought you were.

Spinners! Spinners! Spinners! That's what they're taking. Tie one on and just throw it out there. You can't see it. But the fish can.

Spinner fishing will last until the entire sun is below the horizon, but I should alert you to be ready for Hill's "third rise," during which time you can land the biggest trout of your life. Prepare for this moment by replacing the spinner with a caddis pattern, like my Mother's Day caddis above. Cut back on the leader to at least 6 or 8 lb. breaking strain, or have prepared beforehand a piece of 6 or 8 lb leader with a loop on one end and the caddis on the other for easy attachment to the leader on your line. (It will be quite dark and anything you can do beforehand will help calm your nerves.)

Caddis should be buzzing around you by now or coming down on the surface or slightly above it. On one river they come down in whirling cones which must provide several insects at one bite. The rises out in the river are immense. The outgoing rings in the gloaming seem to be three or four inches high.

Hills suggested pulling the 'sedge' across the surface a few feet. But on a tight, swinging line, the fly is leaving an invisible wake anyway, and it doesn't need pulling. Just try to reach the rings and let the fly pass through them. One fish is all you need.

There's not much time and the rings are slowing down. It's darker than you can imagine and you think you must be crazy to be fishing in such darkness. The rings have stopped. It's quiet and black. And you know it's over.

The End.

# APPENDIX

The spinner patterns in this book were based on actual insects collected by the writer or borrowed from the collection of Dan Gustafson. Some important Eastern spinners were not included in either collection. Based on descriptions, drawings and photographs of some of these species in taxonomic and in fly fishing literature, the following spinner fly patterns are suggested.

Dark Hendrickson Gold Tail™:

Hook: Tiemco 100: 12
Abdomen: Tobacco brown
Thorax: Darker reddish brown
Ribbing: Fine gold wire, several close or solid wraps at tail, then normal spaced to thorax, suggesting an egg sack
Hackle: Light ginger
Tail: Golden pheasant topping barbs

Light Hendrickson Gold Tail™:

Hook: Tiemco 100: 14
Abdomen: Light olive
Thorax: Dark olive
Ribbing: Fine gold wire, several close or solid wraps at tail, then normal spaced to thorax, suggest ing an egg sack
Hackle: Pale ginger, or light dun
Tail: Wood duck flank feather barbs

Blue Winged Olive Gold Tail™:

Hook: Tiemco 100: 16 or 18
Abdomen: Dark olive
Thorax: Dark brown olive
Ribbing: Fine gold wire, several close or solid wraps at tail, then normal spaced to thorax, suggesting an egg sack.
Hackle: Light ginger or rusty edge
Tail: Golden pheasant topping feather

Isonychia sadleri and bicolor Gold Tail™:

Hook: Tiemco 109 BL: 11
Abdomen: Tobacco brown, deeply darkened with Sanford brown marker
Thorax: Dark brown, nearly black
Ribbing: Fine gold wire, several close or solid wraps at tail then normal spaced to thorax, suggesting an egg sack
Hackle: Light ginger or rusty edge
Tail: Golden pheasant topping feather

Epeorus pleuralis (Quill Gordon) Gold Tail™:

Hook: Tiemco 109BL: 11
Abdomen: Biege
Thorax: Light brown
Ribbing: Fine gold wire, several close or solid wraps at tail then normal spaced to thorax, suggesting an egg sack
Hackle: Light ginger or rusty edge
Tail: Golden pheasant topping feather

BIBLIOGRAPHY

Arbona, Fred, L., Jr., Mayflies, The Angler, and the Trout, Winchester Press, Piscataway, NJ, 1980
Berner and Edmunds, Jensen, MAYFLIES OF NORTH AND CENTRAL AMERICA, University of Minnesota Press, Minneapolis, 1976
Berners, Dame Juliana, TREATYSE OF FFYSSHYNGE WITH AN ANGLE, England, 1496
Best, Thomas, A CONCISE TREATISE ON THE ART OF ANGLING, England, 1787
Bowlker, Charles, THE ART OF ANGLING, England, 1829
Caucci, Al and Bob Nastasi, HATCHES, New York, Lyons & Burford, 1975
Dunham, Judith, THE ATLANTIC SALMON FLY, San Francisco, Chronicle Books,1991
Dunne, J. W., SUNSHINE AND THE DRY FLY, A. and C. Black, London, 1924
Eaton, A., E., Reverend, A MONOGRAPH ON THE EPHEMERIDAE, THE TRANSACTIONS OF THE ENTOMOLOGICAL SOCIETY OF LONDON, 1871
Francis, Francis, A BOOK ON ANGLING, Herbert Jenkins Limited, London, 1867
Gustafson, Daniel, ECOLOGY OF AQUATIC INSECTS IN THE GALLATIN RIVER DRAINAGE, Doctorate Paper, Bozeman, MT. 1990
Hafele, Rick and Dave Hughes, THE COMPLETE BOOK OF WESTERN HATCHES, Frank Amato Publications, Portland, 1981
Halford, Frederic, M., DRY-FLY ENTOMOLOGY, England, 1897
-------- DRY-FLY FISHING IN THEORY AND PRACTICE, Sampson Low, Marston, Searle, and Rivington, London, 1889
-------- MODERN DEVELOPMENT OF THE DRY FLY, England, 1910

-------- FLOATING FLIES AND HOW TO DRESS THEM, Sampson Low, Marston, Searle, and Rivington, London, 1886
Harris, J. R., AN ANGLER'S ENTOMOLOGY, COLLINS, 1970
Hills, John Waller, A SUMMER ON THE TEST, Geoffrey Bles, London, 1946
-------- RIVER KEEPER, Geoffrey Bles, 1947
-------- A HISTORY OF FLY FISHING FOR TROUT, Freshet Press, New York, 1971
Leonard, Fannie A., and Justin W. Leonard, MAYFLIES OF MICHIGAN TROUT STREAMS, Cranbrook Institute of Science, Bloomfield Hills, Michigan, 1962
Marinaro, Vincent, A MODERN DRY FLY CODE, Nick Lyons Books, New York, 1970
-------- IN THE RING OF THE RISE, Crown Publishers, New York, 1976
Martin, Darrel, MICROPATTERNS, Lyons and Burford, New York, 1994
McCully, C. B., A DICTIONARY OF FLY-FISHING, Oxford University Press, England, 1993
McDonald, John, THE COMPLETE FLY FISHERMAN, Charles Scribner, New York, 1947
Meck, Charles, R., MEETING AND FISHING THE HATCHES, Winchester Press, New York, 1977
Mottram, J. C., FLY FISHING: SOME NEW ARTS AND MYSTERIES, The Field & Queen, London, N.D.
-------- THOUGHTS ON ANGLING, Herbert Jenkins, London, N.D.
Needham, James, G., Jay R. Traver, and Yin-Chi Hsu, THE BIOLOGY OF MAYFLIES, Comstock Publishing Co., Ithaca, NY.
Nemes, Sylvester, SOFT-HACKLED FLY IMITATIONS, Bozeman, MT, by the author, 1991
Richards, Carl and Doug Swisher, SELECTIVE TROUT, Crown Publishers, New York, 1971
--------TYING THE SWISHER/RICHARDS FLIES, Stackpole Books, Harrisburg, Pa 1980
Schwiebert, Jr., Ernest G., MATCHING THE HATCH, The

Macmillan Company, New York, 1955
Skues, G.E.M., MINOR TACTICS OF THE CHALK STREAM, Adam and Charles Black, London, 1914
-------- THE WAY OF A TROUT WITH A FLY, Adam and Charles Black, London, 1921
Woolley, Roger, MODERN TROUT FLY DRESSING, The Fishing Gazette, England, 1950

# INDEX

(PLEASE NOTE. To save space and time, this index does not include the names of states, countries, cities or names of fly tying materials and their companies.)